GCSE IN A WE...

AUTHOR - ADAM ARNELL

Use this day-by-day listing and the tabs on each page in the book to plan your revision.

TECTONICS

⊘ Earth's layers

The Earth has a layered structure.

Crust
A layer of solid rock between 6km and 90km thick. Temperature increases with depth to 1200 °C

Mantle
A layer of mostly solid rock 2900km thick. Temperature increases with depth from 1000 °C to 5000 °C. The upper layer of the mantle is semi-molten and able to flow.

Outer core
A layer of molten iron and nickel 2100 km thick. Temperature exceeds 5000 °C

Inner core
A ball of iron and nickel, 2800km in diameter, which is solid due to immense pressure. Temperatures reach 5500 °C

⊘ Tectonic plates

The Earth's crust is broken into huge slabs of rock called **tectonic plates**.

Continental crust forms the land and varies from 25km to 90km thick

Tectonic plates consist of oceanic crust and continental crust

Oceanic crust forms the sea bed and varies from 6km to 11km thick

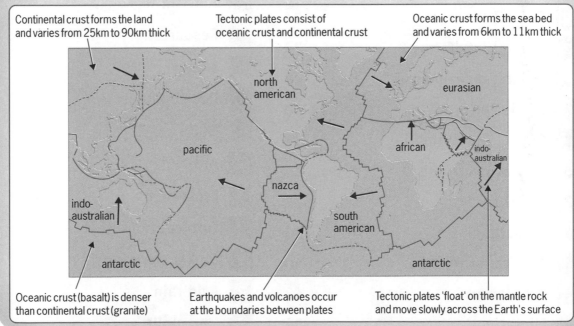

north american

eurasian

pacific

african

indo-australian

indo-australian

nazca

south american

antarctic

antarctic

Oceanic crust (basalt) is denser than continental crust (granite)

Earthquakes and volcanoes occur at the boundaries between plates

Tectonic plates 'float' on the mantle rock and move slowly across the Earth's surface

The Earth seems so solid beneath our feet – but nothing could be further from the truth...

10 MINS

How do tectonic plates move?

The Earth's core is extremely hot due to radioactive processes

Heat from the core rises by convection into the mantle

Convection currents in the top layer of the mantle move in a circular motion

Circular movements 'drag' the tectonic plates, moving them across the Earth's surface

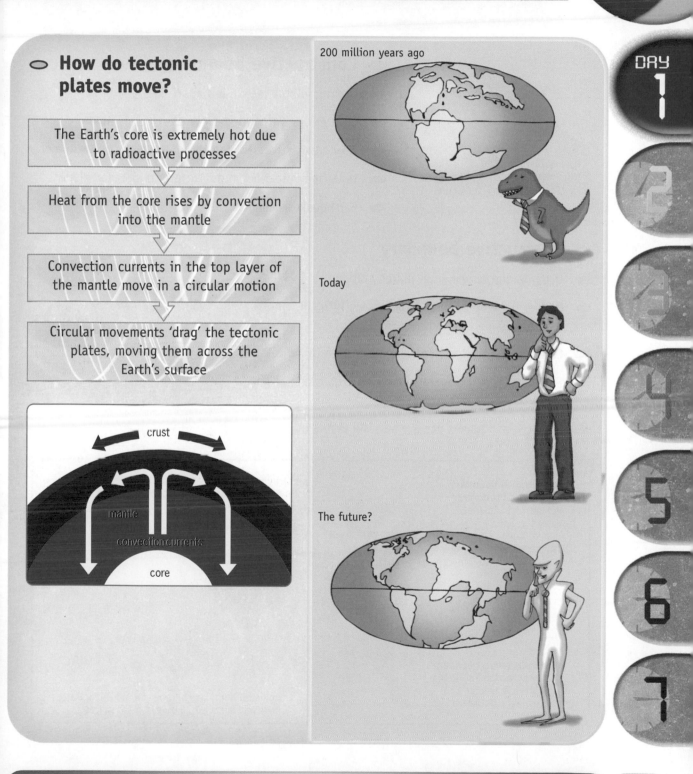

crust

mantle

convection currents

core

200 million years ago

Today

The future?

DAY 1

2
3
4
5
6
7

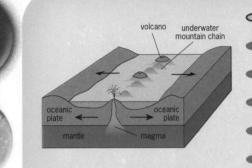

volcano
underwater mountain chain
oceanic plate
oceanic plate
mantle
magma

Constructive boundary

- Oceanic plates are pulled apart
- Lava erupts through the gap that opens up
- New crust is formed and the ocean floor grows larger
- Undersea volcanoes grow to form mid-ocean ridges
- Earthquakes occur as the plates move

Destructive boundary

- Oceanic and continental plates collide
- Denser oceanic crust is forced down into the mantle where it is melted and destroyed
- Continental crust crumples up to form fold mountains
- Explosive volcanoes are formed on either side of the plate boundary
- Strong earthquakes occur when the plates move

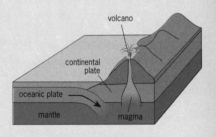

volcano
continental plate
oceanic plate
mantle
magma

Example

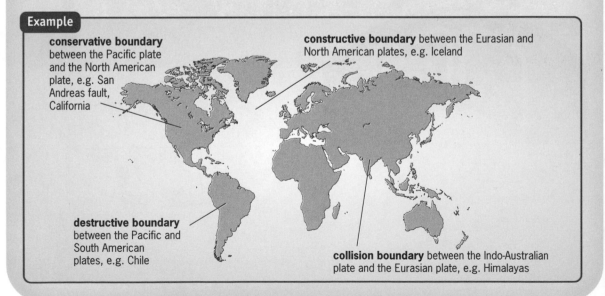

conservative boundary between the Pacific plate and the North American plate, e.g. San Andreas fault, California

constructive boundary between the Eurasian and North American plates, e.g. Iceland

destructive boundary between the Pacific and South American plates, e.g. Chile

collision boundary between the Indo-Australian plate and the Eurasian plate, e.g. Himalayas

Plate boundaries are the places where two or more tectonic plates meet. Plates move together, apart and even sideways past each other.

Collision boundary

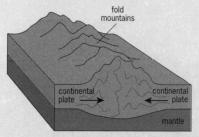

fold mountains

continental plate

continental plate

mantle

- Continental plates collide
- Neither plate is dense enough to sink into the mantle
- Plates crumple together to form fold mountains
- There are powerful earthquakes, but no volcanic eruptions

Conservative boundary

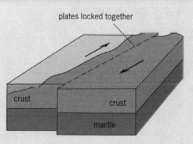

plates locked together

crust

crust

mantle

- Tectonic plates move sideways past each other
- Plates become locked together by friction
- Pressure builds up until the coastal rock snaps along a fault
- Plates move suddenly, causing powerful earthquakes but not volcanoes

Progress check

1 What is a plate boundary?

2 On which two plate boundaries do volcanoes occur?

3 Cross out the incorrect words in the following sentences:

a) A constructive plate boundary's is where two plates are moving **apart/together**.

b) At destructive plate boundaries oceanic crust is **created/destroyed**.

c) Collision boundaries occur where two **oceanic/continental** plates are colliding.

d) Plates move sideways past each other at **destructive/conservative** boundaries.

4 Match the plate boundaries below with the correct example.

a) Constructive	Himalayas
b) Destructive	Iceland
c) Collision	California
d) Conservative	Chile

TEST YOURSELF

DAY 1

What causes earthquakes?

Tectonic plates are locked together by friction

⬇

Pressure builds up due to movement in the mantle

⬇

The rock breaks along a weak point (fault)

⬇

Energy built up over many years is released as seismic waves

⬇

The Earth's surface shakes violently

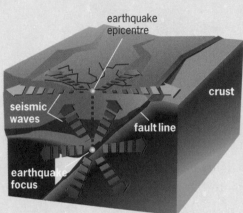

earthquake epicentre

seismic waves

crust

fault line

earthquake focus

What are the impacts of earthquakes?

	Impact	Detail
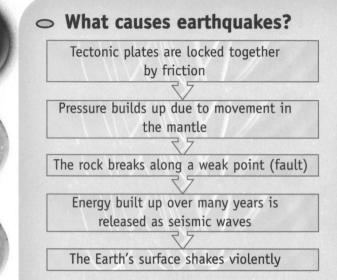	Structural damage	High-rise buildings, houses and bridges may collapse, trapping and killing people
	Falling objects	Glass from broken windows and electricity cables cause injury and death
	Fire	Broken gas pipes may ignite and set fire to buildings. Broken water pipes mean fires are difficult to extinguish
	Tsunami	Coastal areas may be hit by 40-metre-high waves travelling at over 300 miles per hour
	Disease	Cholera and typhoid may break out due to a lack of hygiene if the water supply is affected

Thousands of earthquakes occur each year as the Earth's tectonic plates jostle for position.

DAY 1

Case study

⬭ Gujurat, India (LEDC)

Date: 26 January 2001
Epicentre: Bhuj, Gujurat
Strength: Richter Scale 7.9

Cause:
India is on a collision boundary between the Indian Plate and the Eurasian Plate

Effects:
30 000 dead
55 000 injured
Over 1 million people homeless
Estimated cost £2.2 billion

⬭ Kobe, Japan (MEDC)

Date: 17 January 1995
Epicentre: Awaji Island
Strength: Richter Scale 7.2

Cause:
Japan is on a destructive boundary between the Philippine Plate and the Eurasian Plate

Effects:
5000 dead
30 000 injured
300 000 people homeless
Cost £80 billion

Progress check

1. What is the difference between an earthquake epicentre and focus?

2. Arrange the following statements in order to explain how earthquakes happen:

   a) The Earth's surface shakes
   b) Tectonic plates are locked together by friction
   c) Tectonic plates move
   d) Pressure builds up between two tectonic plates
   e) Crustal rocks snap along a fault line
   f) Stored energy is released

3. What was the cause of the earthquake in Gujurat in 2001?

4. What was the cause of the earthquake in Kobe in 1995?

5. Describe the differing impacts of the earthquakes in Gujurat and Kobe.

VOLCANOES

○ Types of volcano

- **Shield volcano** – wide, gently sloping sides, runny lava

- **Composite volcano** – steep concave sides, layers of ash and lava

- **Acid volcano** – steep convex sides, layers of thick lava

- **Caldera** – huge crater, often filled with a lake

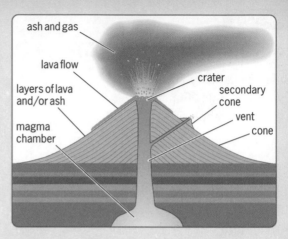

ash and gas

lava flow

layers of lava and/or ash

magma chamber

crater

secondary cone

vent

cone

○ Where do volcanoes occur?

- Destructive plate boundaries – oceanic crust is melted as it is pushed down into the mantle – magma forces its way upwards through the crust

- Constructive plate boundaries – magma rises to fill the gap as two plates pull apart

- Hot spots – chambers of magma develop in the mantle, magma rises and melts through the crust

○ What are the effects of a volcanic eruption?

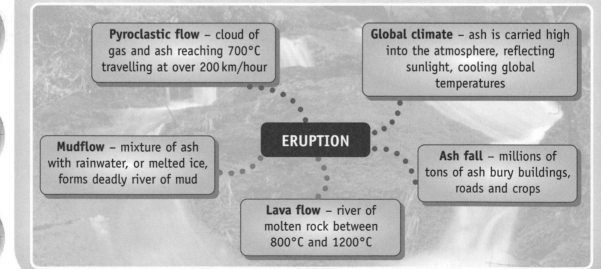

Pyroclastic flow – cloud of gas and ash reaching 700°C travelling at over 200 km/hour

Global climate – ash is carried high into the atmosphere, reflecting sunlight, cooling global temperatures

Mudflow – mixture of ash with rainwater, or melted ice, forms deadly river of mud

ERUPTION

Ash fall – millions of tons of ash bury buildings, roads and crops

Lava flow – river of molten rock between 800°C and 1200°C

Case study

○ Montserrat

Location: Soufriere Hills volcano, Montserrat, Caribbean

Date: eruptions between 1995 and 1997

Cause: Montserrat is on a destructive plate boundary between the South American Plate and the Caribbean Plate. Soufriere Hills is a composite volcano.

Short-term impacts:

- Population evacuated to north of the island
- Pyroclastic flows burned buildings and trees
- Ash over two-thirds of the island

Medium-term impacts:

- 60% of housing destroyed
- Lack of clean water and sewage facilities
- No hospital and few schools remain open

Long-term impacts:

- 8000 people left Montserrat as refugees – only 4000 remain
- Farming impossible as fields are buried under ash
- Tourist industry collapsed
- Coral reefs dying under ash washed into the sea

Progress check

1 Match the descriptions below with the correct term.

a)	Wide	Composite volcano
b)	Steep concave sides	Shield volcano
c)	Steep convex sides	Caldera
d)	Huge crater	Acid volcano

2 Match the descriptions below with the correct term.

a)	River of molten rock	Pyroclastic flow
b)	Cloud of red-hot gas and ash	Mudflow
c)	Pulverised rock and lava falls back down to earth	Lava flow
d)	River of volcanic ash and water	Ash fall

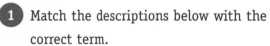

DAY
1
2
4
5
6
7

○ Rock groups

There are three groups of rocks: igneous, sedimentary and metamorphic.

volcanoes

igneous rocks formed from cooled lava (extrusive), e.g. basalt.

sedimentary rocks formed on the sea bed from particles of other rocks, or the remains of plants and animals, e.g. chalk and sandstone

sea

metamorphic rocks formed from igneous or sedimentary rocks by volcanic activity, e.g. marble or slate

igneous rocks formed from cooled magma (intrusive), e.g. granite

○ Describing rocks

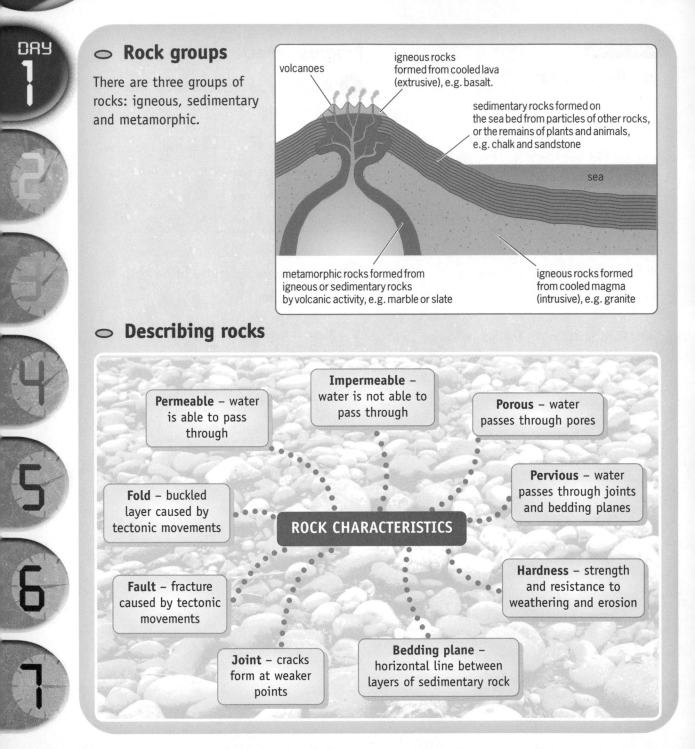

Permeable – water is able to pass through

Impermeable – water is not able to pass through

Porous – water passes through pores

Fold – buckled layer caused by tectonic movements

Pervious – water passes through joints and bedding planes

ROCK CHARACTERISTICS

Fault – fracture caused by tectonic movements

Hardness – strength and resistance to weathering and erosion

Joint – cracks form at weaker points

Bedding plane – horizontal line between layers of sedimentary rock

The layers of solid rocks at the Earth's surface are in a continual cycle of formation and destruction.

10 MINS

Weathering

Weathering is the slow breakdown of rocks by natural processes.

Physical weathering

Freeze–thaw weathering is the break up of rock by ice. Water seeps into a crack when the temperature is above 0°C. If the temperature falls to 0°C, the water turns to ice and expands. Pressure from the expanding ice widens the crack. After many freeze–thaw cycles the rock is shattered into smaller pieces. Pieces of rock build up at the foot of cliffs to form scree slopes.

Chemical weathering

Carbonation is the breakdown of some types of rock by chemical action. Rainwater absorbs carbon dioxide from the atmosphere, forming acidic rain. Acid rainwater dissolves calcium carbonate in chalk and limestone. Limestone weathered by carbonation forms limestone pavements at the surface, and caves underground.

Biological weathering

Biological weathering is the breakdown of rock by vegetation, animals and insects. Trees and plants are able to break up rocks with their roots. As the roots grow and expand they exert pressure on the rock, eventually breaking it in two. Burrowing creatures, such as worms and rabbits, help to break up weak rocks such as clay.

Progress check

1 What type of rock is formed from lava?

2 What type of rock is formed from particles of other rocks?

3 What is the difference between permeable and impermeable rock?

4 What is the difference between a joint and a bedding plane?

5 Arrange the following statements in the correct order to explain freeze–thaw weathering.
a) Ice expands exerting pressure
b) Ice melts
c) Water freezes
d) Water seeps into crack
e) Crack is enlarged

DAY 1
2
3
4
5
6
7

LIMESTONE

What is limestone?

Limestone is a sedimentary rock. It is formed from the fossilised remains of sea creatures that lived millions of years ago. As the creatures died, their shells and skeletons fell to the sea floor. Over many years, they built up in thick layers and were compressed to form new rock. Later, tectonic movements of the Earth's crust lifted the limestone above sea level.

Limestone landforms

Limestone areas are known as **karst landscapes**.

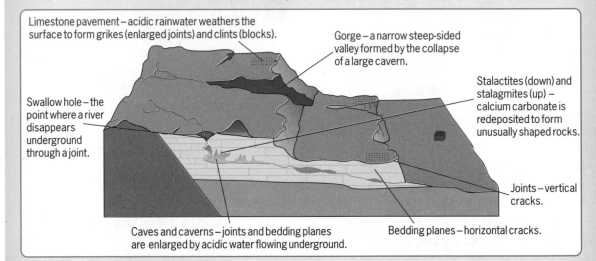

Limestone pavement – acidic rainwater weathers the surface to form grikes (enlarged joints) and clints (blocks).

Gorge – a narrow steep-sided valley formed by the collapse of a large cavern.

Stalactites (down) and stalagmites (up) – calcium carbonate is redeposited to form unusually shaped rocks.

Swallow hole – the point where a river disappears underground through a joint.

Joints – vertical cracks.

Caves and caverns – joints and bedding planes are enlarged by acidic water flowing underground.

Bedding planes – horizontal cracks.

Uses of limestone

- **Building material** – stone is quarried and used in the construction of houses and other buildings.

- **Cement** – limestone is ground into powder and baked for use in construction.

- **Fertiliser** – crushed limestone is added to soil to reduce acidity.

- **Steel industry** – limestone is used to manufacture steel.

- **Farming** – upland areas are suitable for sheep farming.

- **Recreation** – limestone provides excellent opportunities for walking, climbing and caving.

- **Tourism** – dramatic scenery and pretty villages attract sightseers.

Limestone landscapes can form stunning upland areas which are valuable to people for recreation, farming and quarrying.

Case study

Yorkshire Dales

The Yorkshire Dales is an upland area of carboniferous limestone in the north of England in the counties of North Yorkshire and Cumbria.

Yorkshire Dales

Conflicts

Conflicts can arise between different groups of people in limestone areas.

Quarry companies provide jobs, but upset local people and tourists by creating dust and noise, and by damaging the landscape

Tourists bring money into the area but can upset locals by inconsiderate parking and littering

Farmers come into conflict with tourists who wander through their fields disturbing sheep, especially during lambing

RIVER PROCESSES

Erosion

Rivers erode the land in four different ways.

hydraulic power – pressure of fast flowing water, especially on the banks

attrition – stones become smoother, smaller and rounder as they continually smash into each other

corrasion/abrasion – grinding action of stones carried by the river, especially on the bed

corrosion – rocks such as chalk and limestone are dissolved by acidic river water

Transportation

Rivers carry material (load) in four different ways.

solution – salts and minerals are dissolved in the river water, and therefore are not visible

suspension – tiny particles of silt and clay float in the water making the river look cloudy

traction – boulders are rolled along the river bed by the force of the flowing water

saltation – pebbles bounce along the river bed in a leap-frogging motion

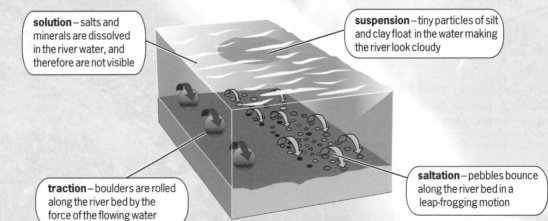

Deposition

The amount a river can carry is controlled by its energy. As a river slows, it loses energy and begins to deposit its load – heaviest first and lightest last. Rivers will deposit material on the inside bend of a meander and at the mouth.

River valley cross-sections

The shape of a river valley changes between the source and the mouth.

Upper valley

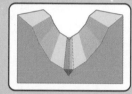

- Narrow V-shaped valley
- Steep valley sides
- River erodes downwards
- Bedload = angular boulders

Middle valley

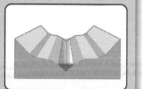

- Wider V-shaped valley
- Gentle valley sides
- River erodes downwards and sideways
- Bedload = smoother pebbles

Lower valley

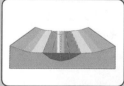

- Wide flat valley
- Very gently sloping valley sides
- River erodes sideways and deposits load
- Bedload = smooth pebbles, sand and silt

Progress check

Match the following descriptions with the correct river processes.

a)	Minerals held in solution in the water	Hydraulic power
b)	Sheer force of flowing water	Abrasion
c)	Silt floats in the water	Corrosion
d)	Pebbles grind against the river bed	Attrition
e)	Boulders roll along the river bed	Traction
f)	River loses energy and drops its load	Saltation
g)	River water dissolves rocks	Erosion
h)	Pebbles smash into each other	Suspension
i)	Pebbles bounce along the river bed	Solution
j)	The river wears away the land	Deposition

15 MINS

V-shaped valley

A steep-sided river valley in an upland area is known as a **V-shaped valley**.

Example

River Tawe, Brecon Beacons, Wales

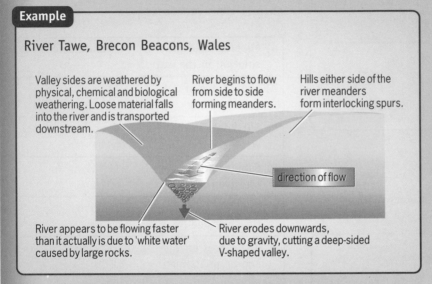

Valley sides are weathered by physical, chemical and biological weathering. Loose material falls into the river and is transported downstream.

River begins to flow from side to side forming meanders.

Hills either side of the river meanders form interlocking spurs.

direction of flow

River appears to be flowing faster than it actually is due to 'white water' caused by large rocks.

River erodes downwards, due to gravity, cutting a deep-sided V-shaped valley.

Meander

A curve in a river is called a **meander**.

Example

River Wear, Durham, England

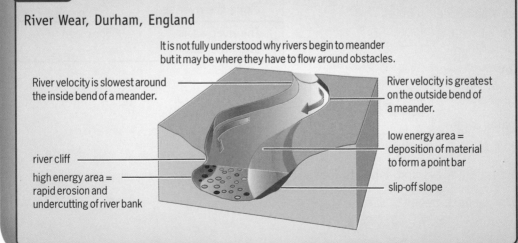

It is not fully understood why rivers begin to meander but it may be where they have to flow around obstacles.

River velocity is slowest around the inside bend of a meander.

River velocity is greatest on the outside bend of a meander.

low energy area = deposition of material to form a point bar

river cliff

high energy area = rapid erosion and undercutting of river bank

slip-off slope

⬭ Waterfall

A point along a river where water drops vertically is called a **waterfall**.

Example

Niagara Falls, USA

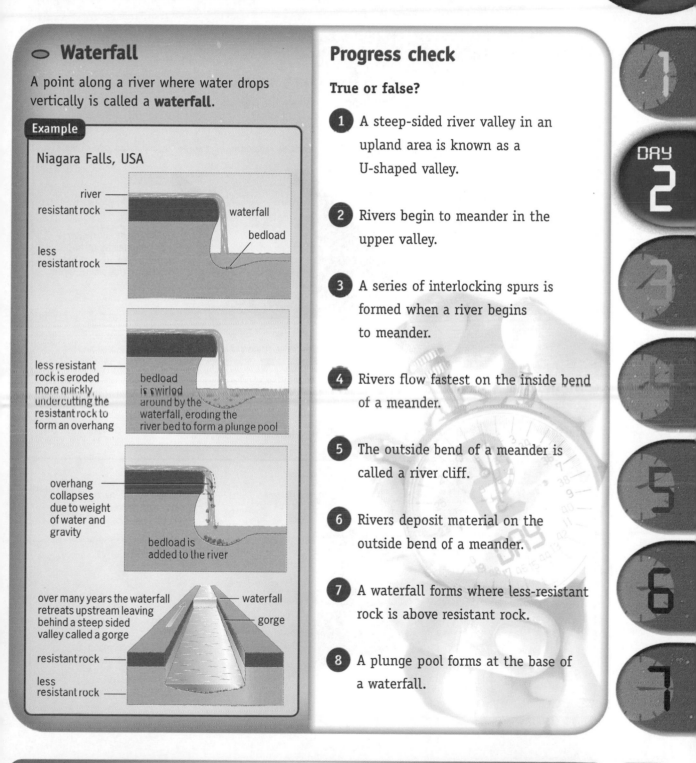

river
resistant rock
waterfall
bedload
less resistant rock

less resistant rock is eroded more quickly, undercutting the resistant rock to form an overhang

bedload is swirled around by the waterfall, eroding the river bed to form a plunge pool

overhang collapses due to weight of water and gravity

bedload is added to the river

over many years the waterfall retreats upstream leaving behind a steep sided valley called a gorge

waterfall
gorge

resistant rock
less resistant rock

Progress check

True or false?

1 A steep-sided river valley in an upland area is known as a U-shaped valley.

2 Rivers begin to meander in the upper valley.

3 A series of interlocking spurs is formed when a river begins to meander.

4 Rivers flow fastest on the inside bend of a meander.

5 The outside bend of a meander is called a river cliff.

6 Rivers deposit material on the outside bend of a meander.

7 A waterfall forms where less-resistant rock is above resistant rock.

8 A plunge pool forms at the base of a waterfall.

RIVER LANDFORMS 2

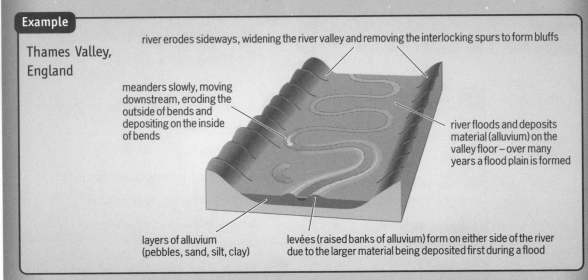

Flood plain and levée

The area of flat land either side of a river is called a **flood plain**.
A **levée** is a raised bank of alluvium along the side of a river.

Example

Thames Valley,
England

river erodes sideways, widening the river valley and removing the interlocking spurs to form bluffs

meanders slowly, moving
downstream, eroding the
outside of bends and
depositing on the inside
of bends

river floods and deposits
material (alluvium) on the
valley floor – over many
years a flood plain is formed

layers of alluvium
(pebbles, sand, silt, clay)

levées (raised banks of alluvium) form on either side of the river
due to the larger material being deposited first during a flood

Delta

A **delta** is an area of low-lying land at the mouth of a river formed as a result of deposition.

Example

Nile delta,
Egypt

river channel splits into
smaller channels called
distributaries

river slows down as it enters
the sea, loses energy
and deposits its load

deltas form in
coastal areas with
shallow seas and
a low tidal range

heaviest material
(boulders) deposited first

lightest material
(clay) deposited last

deposited material builds up
in layers to form a new area of
land called a delta

SPEND 15 MINUTES ON THIS TOPIC

As a river nears the end of its journey, erosion and deposition work together forming flood plains, levées, deltas and ox-bow lakes.

⬭ Ox-bow lake

A horseshoe shaped lake, lying next to a river, is called an **ox-bow lake**.

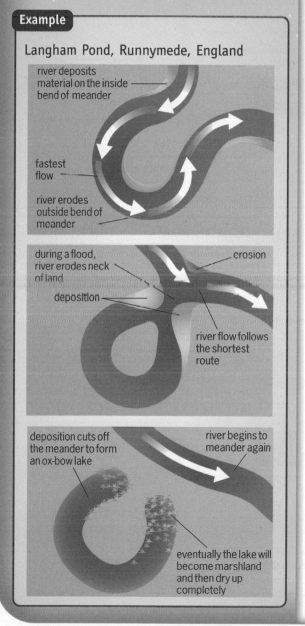

Example

Langham Pond, Runnymede, England

river deposits material on the inside bend of meander

fastest flow

river erodes outside bend of meander

during a flood, river erodes neck of land

erosion

deposition

river flow follows the shortest route

deposition cuts off the meander to form an ox-bow lake

river begins to meander again

eventually the lake will become marshland and then dry up completely

Progress check

Cross out the incorrect words in the sentences below:

a) Rivers **erode/deposit** interlocking spurs to form bluffs.

b) Meanders move very slowly **upstream/downstream**.

c) **Tributaries/distributaries** are found on a delta.

d) A river **loses/gains** energy as it slows down.

e) Rivers deposit the **heaviest/lightest** material last.

f) Rivers **erode/deposit** on the outside bend of a meander.

g) Rivers flow **fastest/slowest** on the outside bend of a meander.

h) Ox-bow lakes are found in the **upper/lower** course of a river.

TEST YOURSELF

19

RIVER FLOODING

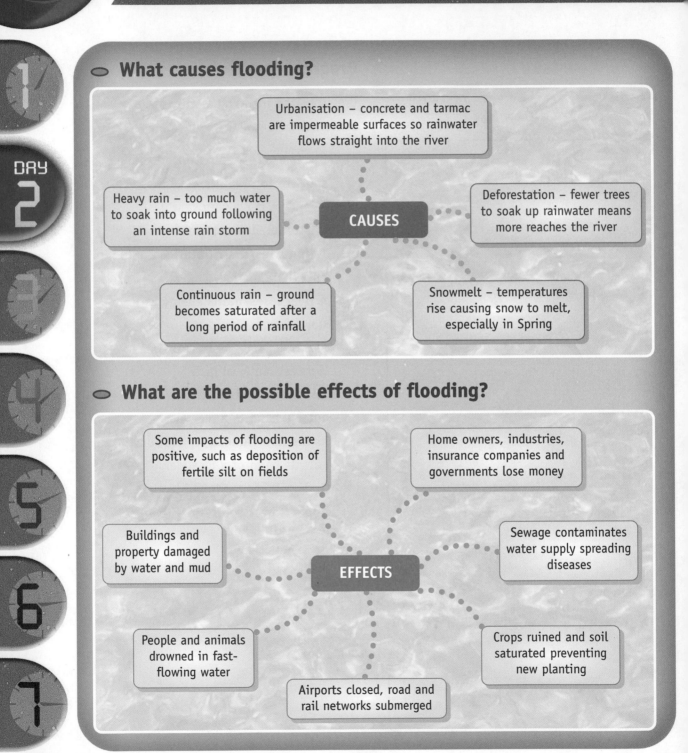

What causes flooding?

Urbanisation – concrete and tarmac are impermeable surfaces so rainwater flows straight into the river

Heavy rain – too much water to soak into ground following an intense rain storm

CAUSES

Deforestation – fewer trees to soak up rainwater means more reaches the river

Continuous rain – ground becomes saturated after a long period of rainfall

Snowmelt – temperatures rise causing snow to melt, especially in Spring

What are the possible effects of flooding?

Some impacts of flooding are positive, such as deposition of fertile silt on fields

Home owners, industries, insurance companies and governments lose money

Buildings and property damaged by water and mud

EFFECTS

Sewage contaminates water supply spreading diseases

People and animals drowned in fast-flowing water

Airports closed, road and rail networks submerged

Crops ruined and soil saturated preventing new planting

A river in flood can be an awesome event that leaves behind a trail of devastation.

10 MINS

Flood management

People try to manage floods.

Dam	Control the amount of water in the river
Levées	Raise banks so river can hold more water
Spillway	Overflow channels allow river to flood onto fields
Afforestation	Plant trees to intercept rainwater
Sandbags	Temporary barriers along river banks and around houses

Case study

Mozambique floods 2000

Location: Mozambique, Africa
Date: February 2000

Causes:
Tropical cyclones caused high winds and heavy rain (1100mm over 4 weeks)
Very large drainage basin brought floodwater from Zambia and Zimbabwe
Dams overflowed, releasing huge amounts of floodwater

Effects:
400 people dead
1 million people homeless
Roads, railways and bridges washed away
Starvation due to loss of food crops
Mosquitoes bred in stagnant water, increasing malaria

Progress check

1 Which of the following is not a cause of flooding?
a) A long period of continuous rain
b) Snow falling in the winter
c) A short period of heavy rain
d) Snow melting in the spring

2 Which of the following is a positive effect of flooding?
a) Buildings damaged by mud
b) Fields covered with silt
c) Water supply contaminated
d) Airports closed

3 Which of the following is a temporary solution to flooding?
a) Sandbags
b) A dam
c) Afforestation
d) A spillway

DAY 2

How does the sea erode the coast?

The sea and waves erode the coast in four ways.

Hydraulic power – waves crash into the cliff compressing air in cracks → the increase in pressure blasts the rock apart.

Corrosion – rocks containing calcium carbonate, such as chalk and limestone, are slowly dissolved by sea water.

Abrasion/corrosion – powerful waves pick up pebbles and hurl them against the cliff, which becomes undercut by the sandblasting effect.

Attrition – pebbles on the beach are rubbed against each other by the waves → over time they become smaller and rounder.

What is longshore drift?

The movement of sand and pebbles along the coast is called **longshore drift**.

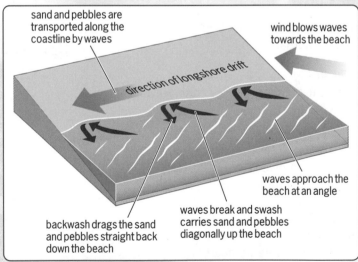

sand and pebbles are transported along the coastline by waves

wind blows waves towards the beach

direction of longshore drift

waves approach the beach at an angle

waves break and swash carries sand and pebbles diagonally up the beach

backwash drags the sand and pebbles straight back down the beach

When does the sea deposit material?

The sea deposits material when waves moving up the beach (**swash**) are more powerful than waves moving down the beach (**backwash**).

10 MINS

Waves

Waves are caused by friction between wind and the surface of the sea – not by the moon!

There are two main types of wave – **constructive** and **destructive**.

- Swash is stronger than backwash
- Waves are long in relation to height

Constructive waves

- Good weather with gentle winds
- Waves deposit material
- Six to ten waves per minute

- Backwash is stronger than swash
- Stormy weather with strong winds

Destructive waves

- Waves are high in relation to length
- Waves erode material
- Eleven to fifteen waves per minute

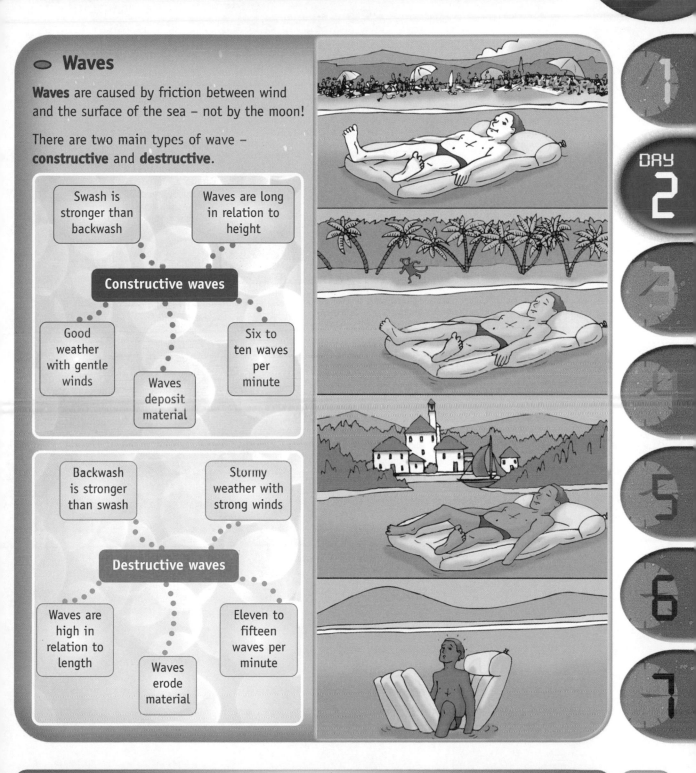

DAY 2

COASTAL LANDFORMS 1

DAY 2

Caves, arches, stacks and stumps

crack – joints and bedding planes in the rock are weathered and eroded

cave – waves pound against the cliffs, eroding and enlarging the cracks to form caves

stack – the top of the arch is weathered, and the bottom is eroded and undercut, until the arch collapses leaving a stack

chemical, physical and biological weathering breaks down the rock

waves erode by hydraulic power and abrasion

arch – caves form on either side of the headland and eventually join together forming an arch

stump – the base of the stack is eroded until it falls over, leaving behind a stump

Case study

Swanage coast, Dorset, England

Cave: Tilly Whim caves
Arch: No Man's Land
Stack: Old Harry
Stump: Old Harry's Wife
Headland: The Foreland
Bay: Swanage Bay

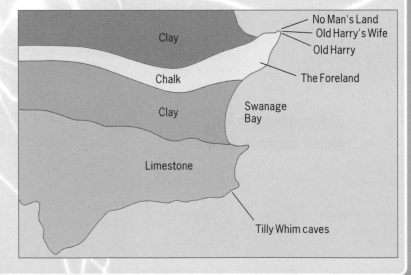

Clay

No Man's Land
Old Harry's Wife
Old Harry

Chalk

The Foreland

Clay

Swanage Bay

Limestone

Tilly Whim caves

Caves, arches, stacks, stumps, headlands and bays are all classic coastal landforms created by wave erosion.

○ Headlands and bays

Headlands and bays form in areas with alternating bands of different rock.

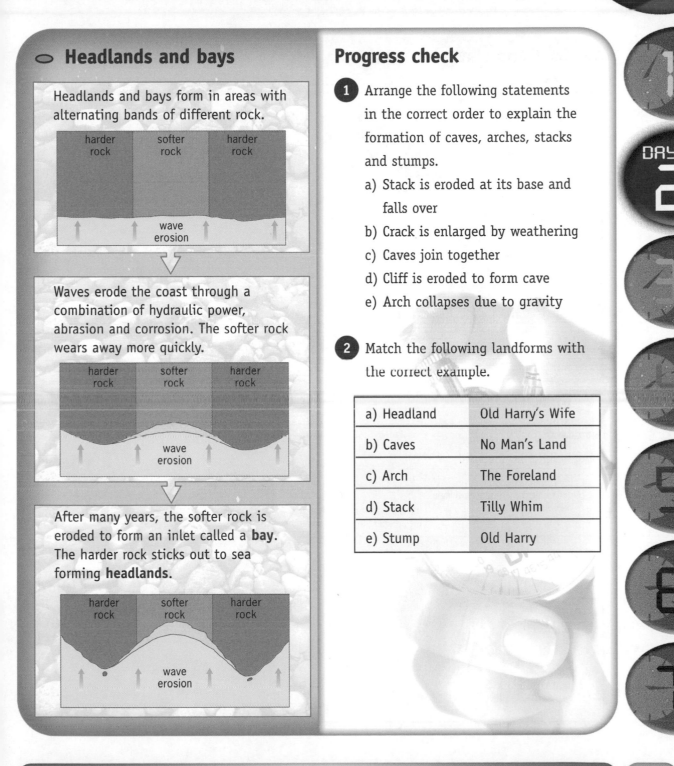

| harder rock | softer rock | harder rock |

wave erosion

Waves erode the coast through a combination of hydraulic power, abrasion and corrosion. The softer rock wears away more quickly.

| harder rock | softer rock | harder rock |

wave erosion

After many years, the softer rock is eroded to form an inlet called a **bay**. The harder rock sticks out to sea forming **headlands**.

| harder rock | softer rock | harder rock |

wave erosion

Progress check

1 Arrange the following statements in the correct order to explain the formation of caves, arches, stacks and stumps.

a) Stack is eroded at its base and falls over

b) Crack is enlarged by weathering

c) Caves join together

d) Cliff is eroded to form cave

e) Arch collapses due to gravity

2 Match the following landforms with the correct example.

a) Headland	Old Harry's Wife
b) Caves	No Man's Land
c) Arch	The Foreland
d) Stack	Tilly Whim
e) Stump	Old Harry

DAY 2

COASTAL LANDFORMS 2

Cliff and wave-cut platform

Example

White cliffs of Dover, England

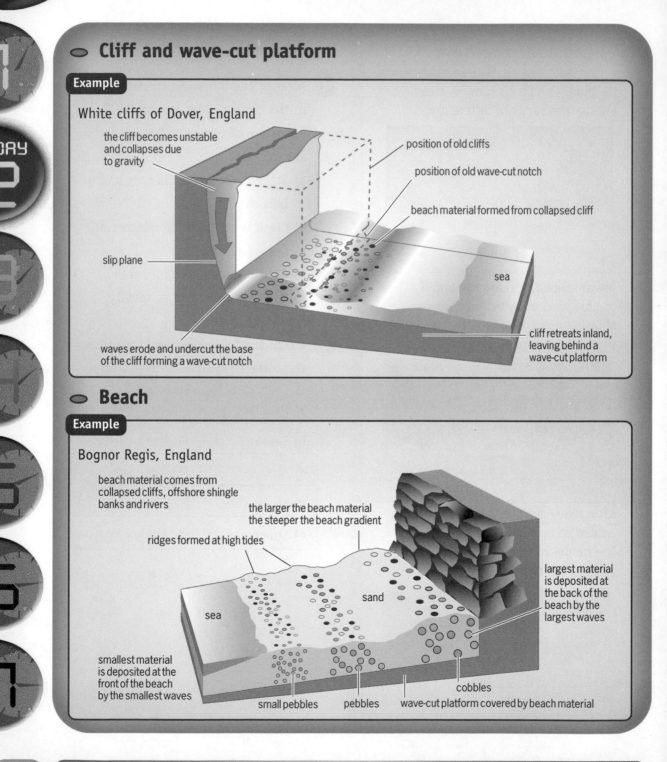

the cliff becomes unstable and collapses due to gravity

position of old cliffs

position of old wave-cut notch

beach material formed from collapsed cliff

slip plane

sea

waves erode and undercut the base of the cliff forming a wave-cut notch

cliff retreats inland, leaving behind a wave-cut platform

Beach

Example

Bognor Regis, England

beach material comes from collapsed cliffs, offshore shingle banks and rivers

the larger the beach material the steeper the beach gradient

ridges formed at high tides

largest material is deposited at the back of the beach by the largest waves

sand

sea

smallest material is deposited at the front of the beach by the smallest waves

small pebbles

pebbles

wave-cut platform covered by beach material

cobbles

15 MINS

⬭ Spit

A **spit** is a curved beach that extends into the sea.

Example

Spurn Head, Holderness coast, England

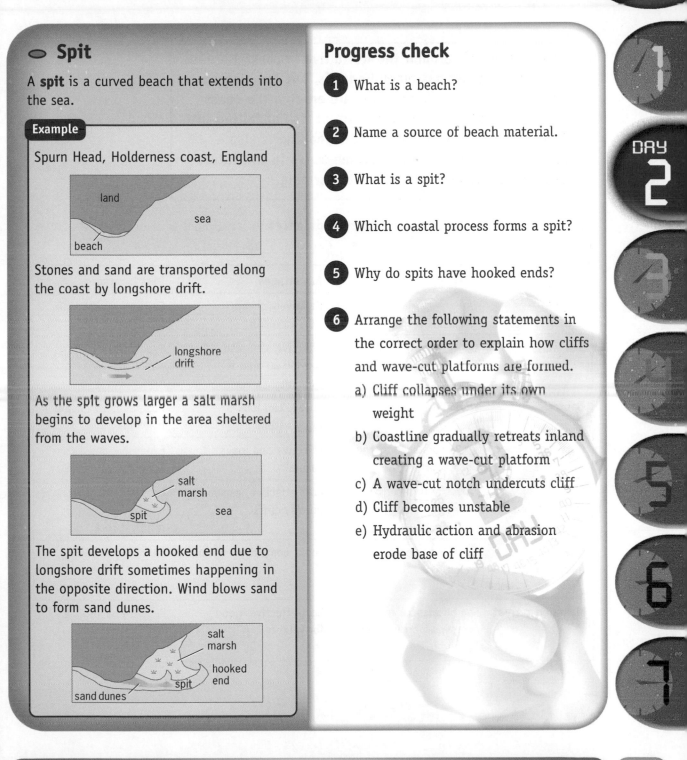

land

sea

beach

Stones and sand are transported along the coast by longshore drift.

longshore drift

As the spit grows larger a salt marsh begins to develop in the area sheltered from the waves.

salt marsh

spit

sea

The spit develops a hooked end due to longshore drift sometimes happening in the opposite direction. Wind blows sand to form sand dunes.

salt marsh

hooked end

spit

sand dunes

Progress check

1 What is a beach?

2 Name a source of beach material.

3 What is a spit?

4 Which coastal process forms a spit?

5 Why do spits have hooked ends?

6 Arrange the following statements in the correct order to explain how cliffs and wave-cut platforms are formed.
   a) Cliff collapses under its own weight
   b) Coastline gradually retreats inland creating a wave-cut platform
   c) A wave-cut notch undercuts cliff
   d) Cliff becomes unstable
   e) Hydraulic action and abrasion erode base of cliff

DAY 2

1
3
5
6
7

COASTAL MANAGEMENT

DAY
3

Millions of people around the world live in coastal areas. Living on the coast has many benefits, but can also be dangerous. In areas where waves are eroding the coast, farmland, houses and industries are at risk of falling into the sea. In low-lying areas, coastal flooding is also a threat. These problems may become worse in the future if sea levels rise because of global warming.

Local authorities are responsible for **coastal defences**. A large number of different strategies may be used.

Strategy	Description	Advantages	Disadvantages
Groyne	Wooden barrier to reduce longshore drift	Relatively cheap, easy to repair	Causes more erosion further down the coast
Sea wall	Concrete wall at the back of the beach	Effective, can also provide an area to walk on	Expensive, can be undercut by waves
Gabion	Wire cage holding rocks together	Cheap, can look fairly natural	Hazardous to people if it fails
Rock armour	Boulders placed at the bottom of cliffs	Effective and looks natural	Expensive and boulders can move
Cliff stabilisation	Cliffs are terraced and drains installed	Cost-effective, especially on clay cliffs	Uses up land and dried out cliffs can result in rock falls
Beach nourishment	Sand and pebbles are added to the beach	Looks completely natural	Short-term solution, seabed ecosystem damaged
Managed retreat	Sea allowed to erode and compensation is given to land owners	Cost-effective, good for wildlife	People lose property

Protecting the coast from erosion is a difficult and expensive business.

15 MINS

Case study

Mappleton, Yorkshire, England

Mappleton is located on the Holderness coastline, which has one of the fastest rates of coastal erosion in the world (average one to two metres a year). The cliffs are made from a very soft rock called till, which crumbles when hit by waves. Mappleton was in danger of falling into the sea until 1991 when the local authority spent £2.1 million on a coastal defence scheme.

Mappleton   cliffs stabilised   rock groyne

direction of longshore drift

rock armour protects cliffs from wave erosion
rock groyne traps sand   beach nourishment provides a natural defence

Has it worked?

The scheme has protected Mappleton very well, but has caused problems elsewhere. Previously, sand and pebbles were moved along the coast by longshore drift. Today they are trapped by the groynes. This means that cliffs 3km to the south are no longer well protected by a beach. At high tide the waves reach the base of the cliffs and erosion has increased to 10 metres a year. Farmers have lost land and homes.

Progress check

1 Who is responsible for managing the UK's coastline?

2 Why may coastal flooding increase in the future?

3 Where is Mappleton?

4 How much was spent on protecting Mappleton?

5 Why were the Mappleton coastal defences not totally effective?

6 Match the descriptions below with the correct type of coastal management.

a) Large erosion-resistant boulders	Groyne
b) A wooden barrier jutting into the sea	Cliff stabilisation
c) Dumping sand and pebbles on a beach	Managed retreat
d) Cutting steps into steep cliffs	Rock armour
e) Land is eroded and allowed to flood	Beach nourishment

DAY 3

GLACIATION

Ice ages

An ice age is a cooling in the average temperature of the Earth by about 5°C. The last ice age began 80 000 years ago. Ice sheets and glaciers grew out from the North Pole and South Pole to cover 30% of the Earth. In the UK, glaciers grew as far as South Wales, the Midlands and Norfolk. The ice age ended 10 000 years ago when the glaciers melted.

limit of ice during last glacial period

Glaciers

A **glacier** is a slow-moving river of ice that forms in upland areas.
Today, glaciers are still found in mountainous areas such as the Alps, Rockies and Himalayas.

Example

Athabasca Glacier, Alberta, Canada

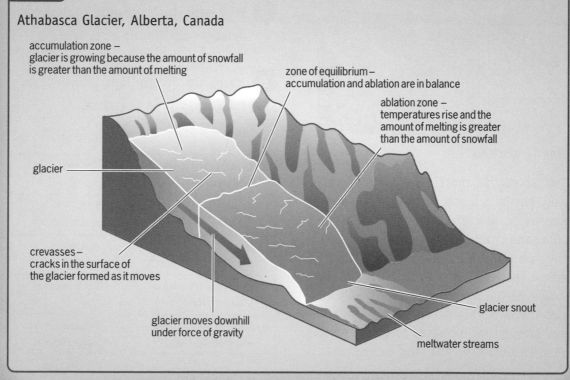

accumulation zone – glacier is growing because the amount of snowfall is greater than the amount of melting

zone of equilibrium – accumulation and ablation are in balance

ablation zone – temperatures rise and the amount of melting is greater than the amount of snowfall

glacier

crevasses – cracks in the surface of the glacier formed as it moves

glacier moves downhill under force of gravity

glacier snout

meltwater streams

Ice ages are surprisingly rare, but when they happen they have a dramatic impact on the Earth's landscape.

15 MINS

How do glaciers move?

Glaciers move downhill an average of two metres per day – but the fastest is moving at 35 metres per day (Columbia Glacier, USA).

Glaciers move by:

- **Slippage** – glacier slides over meltwater
- **Deformation** – glacier bends and flows
- **Melting** – glacier melts and then re-freezes

How do glaciers erode?

Glaciers have massive erosive power. As they slide downhill they carve through the land by a combination of freeze–thaw action, plucking and abrasion.

Freeze–thaw action

Water seeps into cracks in the rock beneath the glacier when the temperature is above 0°C. The temperature falls below 0°C and the water freezes. As it turns to ice it expands and fractures the rock into fragments.

Plucking

Ice at the base and sides of the glacier melts during the daytime. At night, the water freezes around fragments of rock loosened by freeze–thaw action. As the glacier moves downhill it pulls away the fragments.

Abrasion

Fragments of rock that have been 'plucked' by the glacier become embedded in the base and sides. As the glacier moves, the rocks erode the surrounding valley by scratching and grinding.

Progress check

1. What is a glacier?

2. What is the accumulation zone?

3. What is the ablation zone?

4. Name three ways that glaciers move.

5. Name three ways that glaciers erode.

6. Complete the following sentences using the words below:

   a) An ice age is an average global cooling of ... degrees Celcius.

   b) The last ice age began ... thousand years ago.

   c) During the last ice age ... percent of the Earth was covered in ice.

   d) The most recent ice age ended ... thousand years ago.

   e) On average, glaciers move ... metres a day.

   | two | five | thirty | eighty | ten |

DAY **3**

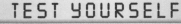

10 MINS

DAY 3

● Upland glacial landforms

A **corrie** is a deep, circular hollow.
An **arête** is a steep-sided ridge.
A **pyramidal peak** is a sharp, pointed mountain summit.

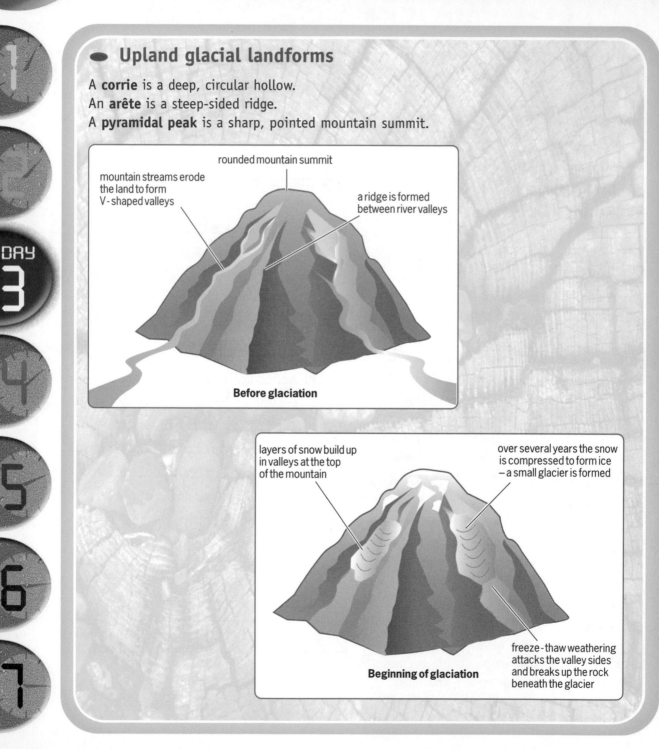

rounded mountain summit

mountain streams erode
the land to form
V-shaped valleys

a ridge is formed
between river valleys

Before glaciation

layers of snow build up
in valleys at the top
of the mountain

over several years the snow
is compressed to form ice
– a small glacier is formed

Beginning of glaciation

freeze-thaw weathering
attacks the valley sides
and breaks up the rock
beneath the glacier

Corries, arêtes and pyramidal peaks are all upland glaciated landforms.

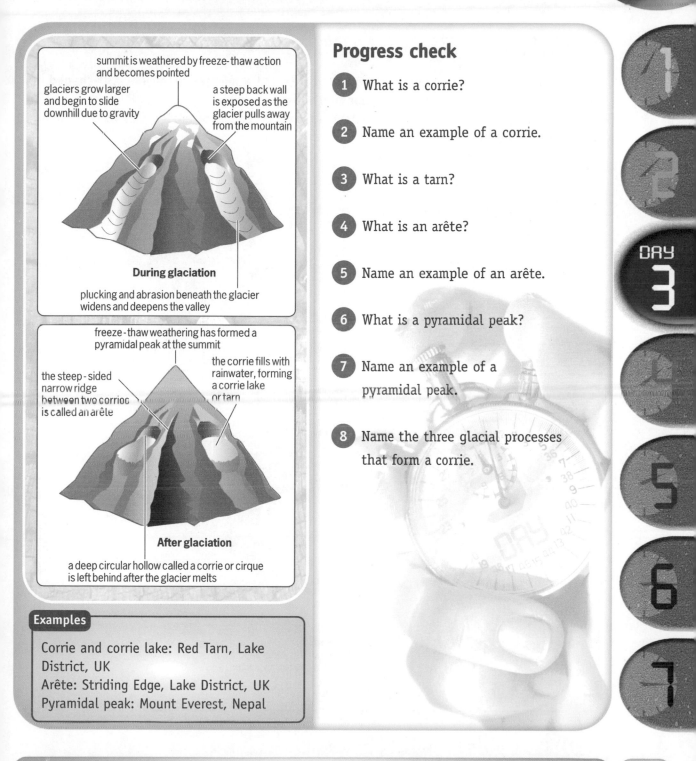

summit is weathered by freeze-thaw action and becomes pointed

glaciers grow larger and begin to slide downhill due to gravity

a steep back wall is exposed as the glacier pulls away from the mountain

During glaciation

plucking and abrasion beneath the glacier widens and deepens the valley

freeze-thaw weathering has formed a pyramidal peak at the summit

the steep-sided narrow ridge between two corries is called an arête

the corrie fills with rainwater, forming a corrie lake or tarn

After glaciation

a deep circular hollow called a corrie or cirque is left behind after the glacier melts

Examples

Corrie and corrie lake: Red Tarn, Lake District, UK

Arête: Striding Edge, Lake District, UK

Pyramidal peak: Mount Everest, Nepal

Progress check

1 What is a corrie?

2 Name an example of a corrie.

3 What is a tarn?

4 What is an arête?

5 Name an example of an arête.

6 What is a pyramidal peak?

7 Name an example of a pyramidal peak.

8 Name the three glacial processes that form a corrie.

GLACIAL LANDFORMS 2

● U-shaped valley

As a glacier flows from its source in a corrie it carves out a massive, steep-sided, **U-shaped valley**. This is often joined by smaller **hanging valleys**.

At the end of the ice age the glacier melts and retreats, depositing eroded rock (till) to form **moraines** and **drumlins**.

Example

Great Langdale Valley, Lake District, England

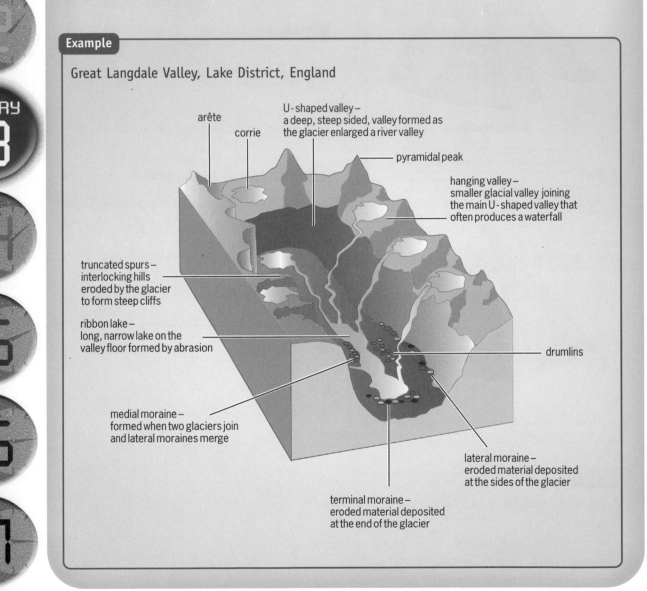

arête

corrie

U-shaped valley –
a deep, steep sided, valley formed as
the glacier enlarged a river valley

pyramidal peak

hanging valley –
smaller glacial valley joining
the main U-shaped valley that
often produces a waterfall

truncated spurs –
interlocking hills
eroded by the glacier
to form steep cliffs

ribbon lake –
long, narrow lake on the
valley floor formed by abrasion

drumlins

medial moraine –
formed when two glaciers join
and lateral moraines merge

lateral moraine –
eroded material deposited
at the sides of the glacier

terminal moraine –
eroded material deposited
at the end of the glacier

● Drumlins

Drumlins are long, narrow, egg-shaped hills found on the valley floor in glaciated areas.

How are drumlins formed?

> The glacier becomes overloaded with eroded rock (till)

> Friction from the valley floor causes the glacier to deposit the till

> The glacier continues to flow over the top of the till

> The till is moulded and shaped – the blunt end points in the direction the glacier came from

Example

Eden Valley, Cumbria

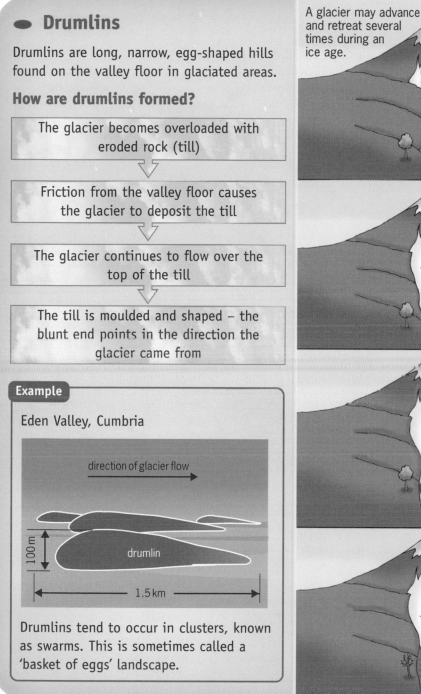

direction of glacier flow

100 m

drumlin

1.5 km

Drumlins tend to occur in clusters, known as swarms. This is sometimes called a 'basket of eggs' landscape.

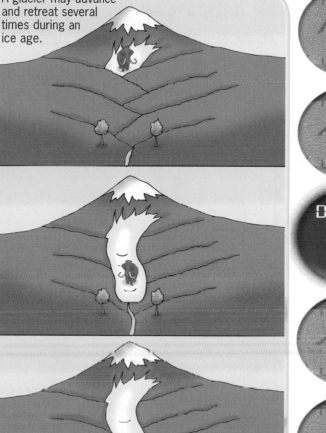

A glacier may advance and retreat several times during an ice age.

DAY
3

Anticyclones

An **anticyclone** is a high-pressure air mass that brings dry, settled weather.

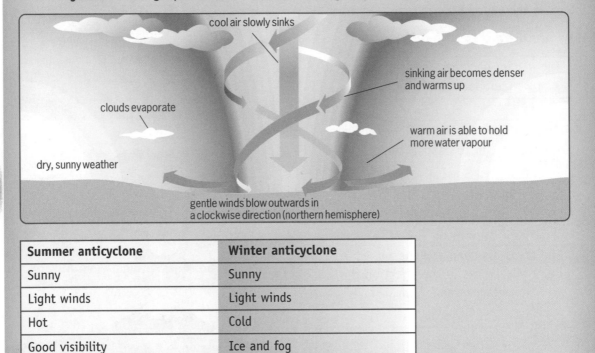

cool air slowly sinks

sinking air becomes denser and warms up

clouds evaporate

warm air is able to hold more water vapour

dry, sunny weather

gentle winds blow outwards in a clockwise direction (northern hemisphere)

Summer anticyclone	Winter anticyclone
Sunny	Sunny
Light winds	Light winds
Hot	Cold
Good visibility	Ice and fog

Depressions

A **depression** is an area of low pressure formed when a warm air mass and a cool air mass meet. Depressions bring wet and windy weather.

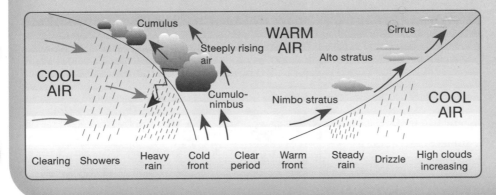

Cumulus

WARM AIR

Cirrus

Steeply rising air

Alto stratus

COOL AIR

Cumulo-nimbus

Nimbo stratus

COOL AIR

| Clearing | Showers | Heavy rain | Cold front | Clear period | Warm front | Steady rain | Drizzle | High clouds increasing |

Weather is the constantly changing conditions of the atmosphere – air pressure, temperature, clouds, rain and wind.

Precipitation

Precipitation includes rain, sleet, hail and snow. Precipitation is formed in three different ways.

Relief

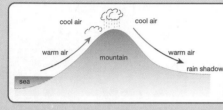

cool air · cool air · warm air · warm air · mountain · rain shadow · sea

Warm, moist air is forced to rise over hills. As it rises it cools, condenses and rains. As the air passes down the other side of the hill the process is reversed. The air warms and clouds evaporate.

Frontal

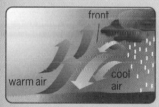

front · warm air · cool air

Warm, moist air collides with cool dry air. The two will not mix because they are different densities. The cool air undercuts the warm air, forcing it to rise. As it rises it cools, condenses and rains.

Convectional

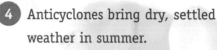

sun · lightning · cool air · warm air

Convectional rainfall happens on hot days. Heat from the sun warms the Earth's surface. Warm air rises rapidly, cools, condenses and forms storm clouds. Heavy rain, and often thunder and lightning, follow.

Progress check

True or false?

1. An anticyclone is a high-pressure air mass.

2. Anticyclones bring wet, windy weather in winter.

3. Anticyclones blow anticlockwise in the northern hemisphere.

4. Anticyclones bring dry, settled weather in summer.

5. Depressions are formed when a warm air mass meets a cool air mass.

6. Cool air rises over warm air in a depression.

7. Depressions bring wet and windy weather in summer.

8. Relief rainfall is caused by air rising over mountains.

9. Frontal rainfall happens when warm and cool air mix together.

10. Convectional rainfall is common in winter.

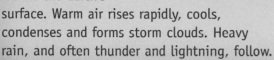

CLIMATE

● Factors affecting climate

Distance from sea

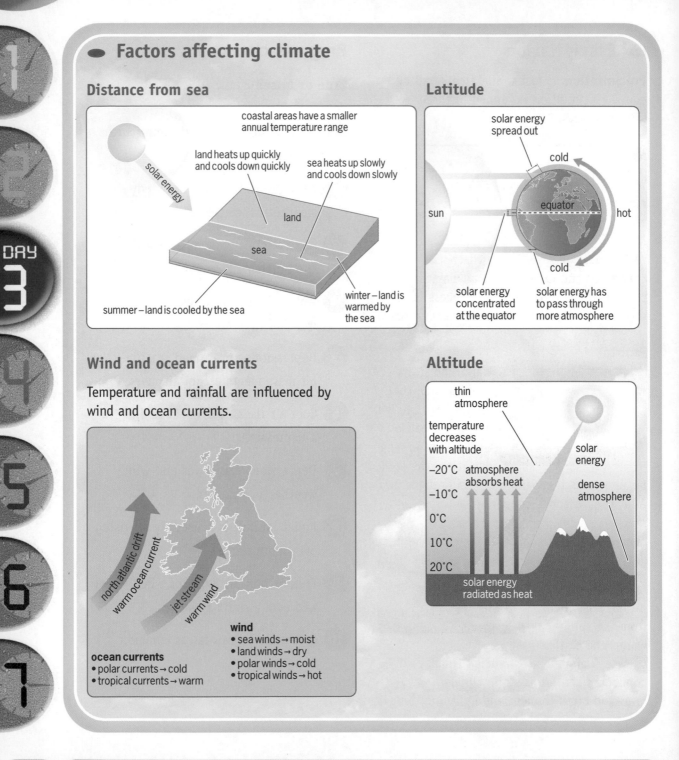

coastal areas have a smaller annual temperature range

land heats up quickly and cools down quickly

sea heats up slowly and cools down slowly

solar energy

land

sea

summer – land is cooled by the sea

winter – land is warmed by the sea

Latitude

solar energy spread out

cold

sun

equator

hot

cold

solar energy concentrated at the equator

solar energy has to pass through more atmosphere

Wind and ocean currents

Temperature and rainfall are influenced by wind and ocean currents.

north atlantic drift
warm ocean current

jet stream
warm wind

ocean currents
• polar currents → cold
• tropical currents → warm

wind
• sea winds → moist
• land winds → dry
• polar winds → cold
• tropical winds → hot

Altitude

thin atmosphere

temperature decreases with altitude

solar energy

−20°C   atmosphere absorbs heat

−10°C

dense atmosphere

0°C

10°C

20°C

solar energy radiated as heat

Weather is constantly changing, but over time a pattern emerges. This average pattern of weather is known as climate.

Global climates

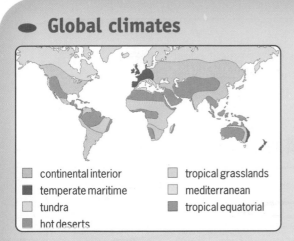

- ☐ continental interior
- ■ temperate maritime
- ☐ tundra
- ■ hot deserts
- ☐ tropical grasslands
- ☐ mediterranean
- ■ tropical equatorial

Tropical equatorial – hot all year (average 27°C); rains every day (average 2000mm per year).

Tropical grassland – hot all year (average 25°C). Has a wet season and a dry season (average 1000mm per year).

Hot desert – very hot all year (average 30°C). Temperatures may exceed 50°C in the day and fall below 0°C at night. Rainfall is unreliable (less than 250mm per year).

Mediterranean – hot in summer (average 25°C), and mild in winter (average 13°C). Rains mainly in the winter (average 500mm per year).

Continental interior – hot in summer (average 20°C), cold in winter (average -15°C). Rains mainly in the summer (average 500mm per year).

Temperate maritime – warm in summer (average 16°C) and mild in winter (average 7°C). Rains all year (average 1000mm per year).

Tundra – short cool summer (average 3°C). A long cold winter (average -28°C). Very low precipitation (average 100mm per year).

Progress check

1 What is climate?

2 Match the descriptions below with the correct climate type.

a)	Very hot and dry all year	Tropical equatorial
b)	Hot all year and rains every day	Tropical grassland
c)	Cool in summer and very cold in winter	Hot desert
d)	Hot all year with a wet season and a dry season	Mediterranean
e)	Hot in summer and mild in winter	Continental interior
f)	Hot in summer and cold in winter	Temperate maritime
g)	Warm in summer and mild in winter	Tundra

DAY
3

TROPICAL STORMS

● What is a tropical storm?

A **tropical storm** is a huge depression that forms over tropical oceans when sea temperatures exceed 27°C. When the wind speed exceeds 74 mph the storms are described as hurricanes, cyclones, typhoons or willy willys, depending on where in the world they are.

Tropical storms may be as large as 500 km wide and last between one and two weeks.

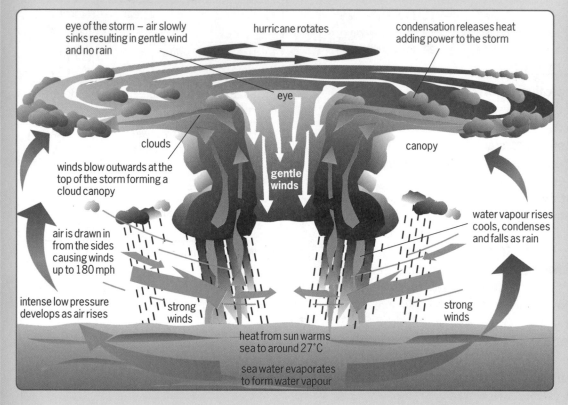

eye of the storm – air slowly sinks resulting in gentle wind and no rain

hurricane rotates

condensation releases heat adding power to the storm

eye

clouds

canopy

winds blow outwards at the top of the storm forming a cloud canopy

gentle winds

water vapour rises cools, condenses and falls as rain

air is drawn in from the sides causing winds up to 180 mph

intense low pressure develops as air rises

strong winds

strong winds

heat from sun warms sea to around 27°C

sea water evaporates to form water vapour

When a tropical storm reaches land it can cause great damage. Strong winds damage buildings, power cables and crops. Heavy rainfall causes flooding and landslides. Intense low pressure allows the sea to rise by over five metres, causing coastal flooding.

Case study

● Hurricane Mitch

Hurricane Mitch, with winds reaching 180 mph, was the deadliest Atlantic hurricane in more than 200 years. It struck Central America in September 1998. In just over a week it caused the deaths of more than 11 000 people, made 3 million people homeless and caused $5 billion-worth of damage.

Impacts of Hurricane Mitch

Honduras:	6500 dead 11 000 missing 1.5 million homeless 70% crop lost
Nicaragua:	3800 dead 7000 missing 800 000 homeless 30% coffee crop lost
El Salvador:	230 dead 500 000 homeless 80% maize crop lost
Guatemala:	200 dead 80 000 evacuated

Progress check

Complete the following sentences using the words below:

a) Tropical storms develop when sea temperatures reach ... degrees Celcius.

b) A tropical storm becomes a hurricane when wind speeds reach ... miles per hour.

c) Tropical storms may have a diameter of ... kilometres.

d) Tropical storms may last for up to ... weeks.

e) Wind speeds in a tropical storm may reach ... miles per hour.

f) Hurricane Mitch was responsible for ... deaths.

g) Hurricane Mitch made ... people homeless.

h) Hurricane Mitch caused ... billion dollars worth of damage.

twenty-seven	five
seventy-four	one hundred and eighty
five hundred	two
three million	eleven thousand

Population density

Population density describes how crowded an area is. It is written as the average number of people per square kilometre. Population density is calculated by dividing the total population of a place by its area in square kilometres.

$$\frac{\text{population}}{\text{area (km}^2)} = \text{population density (km}^2)$$

- An area that has more than 100 people per km^2 is described as being densely populated (crowded).

- An area which has less than 10 people per km^2 is described as being sparsely populated (empty).

Population density

Area	People per km^2
World	43
UK	237
Australia	2
USA	29
China	139

Population distribution

Population distribution describes how the world's people are spread out around the world. The most densely populated areas are Western Europe, India and China. The most sparsely populated areas are North America, South America, Africa and Australia. A number of factors help to explain this pattern of population distribution. Positive factors encourage people to live in an area, while negative factors discourage them.

Explaining population distribution

Factor	Positive ☺	Negative ☹
Relief	Flat land	Mountainous land
Climate	Warm, enough rain	Very hot, very cold, too dry
Vegetation	Open grassland	Dense forest
Soils	Deep, fertile soil	Thin, infertile soil
Resources	Coal, minerals, timber	Few natural resources
Access	Coastal areas	Inland areas
Economy	Plenty of industry and jobs	Lack of industry and jobs

The world's population has reached 6 billion and is still growing – where will everybody live?

Population growth

The rapid increase in global population has been called the 'population explosion'. Throughout most of human history the world's population level was stable.

- Two thousand years ago the population was only 300 million.

- In 1800 the population reached one billion.

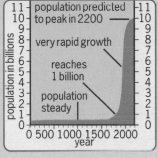

- In the last 200 years the population has increased by six times.

- Population is predicted to peak at 10.4 billion in 2200.

Birth and death rates

Population growth is a complex issue, but basically it is happening because more people are being born than are dying.

- **Birth rate** – the number of babies born per thousand people each year

- **Death rate** – the number of people dying per thousand people each year

When birth rates exceed death rates there is a **natural increase** in population.

Classifying migration

Migration can be classified in different ways.

Immigration – movement into a country	Emigration – movement out of a country
Internal – same country	International – between countries
Permanent – will stay for good	Temporary – will return home again
Voluntary – own choice	Forced – no choice

Push and pull factors

The reasons for migration can be divided into push and pull factors.

- **Push factors** are things about the migrant's place of origin that encourage, or force, people to leave.

- **Pull factors** are things about the migrant's destination that attract them.

Rural to urban migration

In LEDCs people are moving from the countryside to the cities.

Push:
- Few jobs
- Poor wages
- Poor healthcare
- Lack of schools

Pull:
- Jobs
- Higher wages
- Hospitals
- Schools

Impacts:
- Rural depopulation
- Population dominated by young and elderly
- Food production declines

Impacts:
- Jobs hard to find
- Services overstretched
- Squatter settlements grow larger

44

Migration, the movement of people from one place to another, is an increasingly controversial topic.

15 MINS

Urban to rural migration

In MEDCs people are moving from cities to the countryside.

Push:
- Lack of open space
- Air pollution
- Crime

Pull:
- Attractive environment
- Larger houses
- Safer

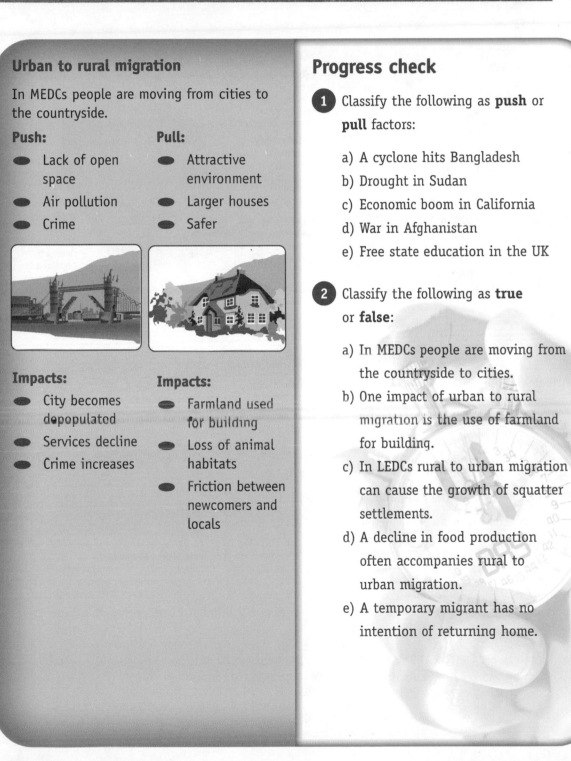

Impacts:
- City becomes depopulated
- Services decline
- Crime increases

Impacts:
- Farmland used for building
- Loss of animal habitats
- Friction between newcomers and locals

Progress check

1 Classify the following as **push** or **pull** factors:

a) A cyclone hits Bangladesh
b) Drought in Sudan
c) Economic boom in California
d) War in Afghanistan
e) Free state education in the UK

2 Classify the following as **true** or **false**:

a) In MEDCs people are moving from the countryside to cities.
b) One impact of urban to rural migration is the use of farmland for building.
c) In LEDCs rural to urban migration can cause the growth of squatter settlements.
d) A decline in food production often accompanies rural to urban migration.
e) A temporary migrant has no intention of returning home.

DAY 4

1 2 3 5 6 7

SETTLEMENT

Site and situation

Site is the exact location of a settlement. Site factors are the physical qualities of the area that were important when the settlement was established. Today, many of the site factors are no longer important.

Situation is the location of a settlement in relation to the surrounding area. A settlement with good access to natural resources and other settlements will grow larger.

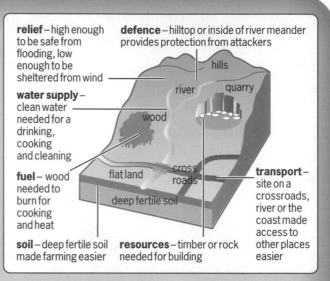

relief – high enough to be safe from flooding, low enough to be sheltered from wind

defence – hilltop or inside of river meander provides protection from attackers

hills

river

quarry

water supply – clean water needed for a drinking, cooking and cleaning

wood

fuel – wood needed to burn for cooking and heat

flat land

cross roads

deep fertile soil

transport – site on a crossroads, river or the coast made access to other places easier

soil – deep fertile soil made farming easier

resources – timber or rock needed for building

What is a settlement hierarchy?

Settlements can be arranged in order of importance – a hierarchy.
Three criteria are used to decide the hierarchy:

- Population size
- Range and number of services
- Distance from other settlement of the same size

The size of a settlement is hard to measure and is NOT used.

Settlement hierarchies can be shown using a pyramid.

importance of settlements

mega-city

city

town

village

hamlet

number of settlements –
one mega-city, thousands of hamlets

- Mega-cities (population over 10 million) are placed at the top of the pyramid because they have the highest population, a huge range and number of services and will be a long way from any other mega-cities.

- Hamlets are placed at the bottom of the pyramid because they have very few people, possibly no services and they will be close to other hamlets.

Sphere of influence

The **sphere of influence** (catchment area) means the area served by a settlement. The sphere of influence is worked out by the range and threshold of services.

Range is the maximum distance people are prepared to travel to use a service.

- Goods bought frequently are called convenience goods, e.g. people will only travel a short distance to do their weekly shopping.

town

——————	newsagent
— — — —	cinema
- - - - -	hospital

- Goods bought infrequently are called comparison goods, e.g. people are prepared to travel further to buy items such as clothing.

Threshold is the minimum number of people needed to support a service.

- Shops selling convenience goods have low threshold populations.

- Shops selling comparison goods have high threshold populations.

The larger the settlement, the greater the number of services and the wider its sphere of influence.

Progress check

1. What is meant by the term 'settlement site'?

2. What is meant by the term 'settlement situation'?

3. Paris is the capital of France and is a mega-city. Classify the following information into **site factors** or **situation factors**:

   a) Paris is centre of European rail network
   b) Island in River Seine provided crossing point
   c) Island location provided good defence
   d) Paris is a focus of road network
   e) River Seine provided water supply
   f) River flood plain provided fertile soil
   g) International airport provides global links
   h) Forest provided fuel supply and building materials

Simplified models have been developed to describe and explain the patterns of land use in both MEDCs and LEDCs.

More Economically Developed Countries (MEDCs)

Concentric circle model (Burgess)

- City grows outwards from the centre in a series of rings.

- Oldest buildings are in the centre, and the newest ones on the outskirts.

- Model does not take account of physical geography or transport links.

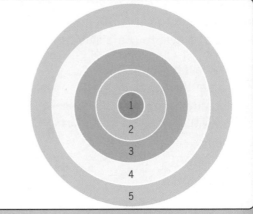

Sector model (Hoyt)

- City grows outwards from centre in rings and sectors.

- Houses built alongside main roads for good accessibility.

- Factories built along railways and canals to enable movement of goods.

- Building takes place on flattest land as it is cheaper to build on.

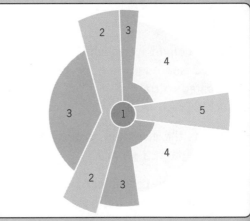

Key
1 Central Business District (CBD) – today shops and offices have replaced factories in the city centre: this is the most expensive land because it is the most accessible
2 Transition zone – old housing, abandoned industry and derelict land surrounds the CBD: the CBD and transition zone together are known as the 'inner city'
3 Low-cost housing – old terraced houses or tower blocks
4 Medium-cost housing – semi-detached houses and renovated terraced houses
5 High-cost housing – semi-detached and detached housing in the suburbs

Less Economically Developed Countries (LEDCs)

Cities in LEDCs have developed differently, in some ways, to those in MEDCs.

- They have expanded more rapidly and in a less managed way.
- The quality of buildings gets worse towards the outskirts.
- Migrants to the cities build their own low-quality housing from scrap materials.

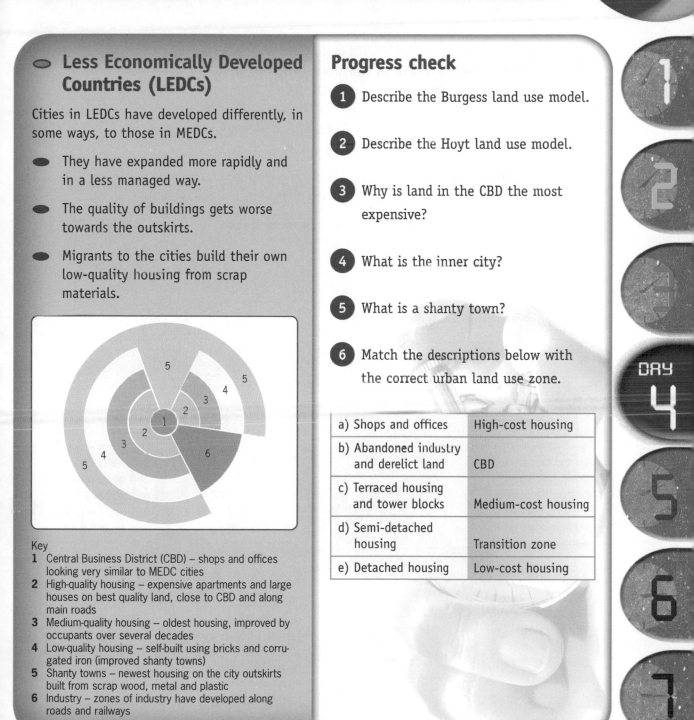

Key
1 Central Business District (CBD) – shops and offices looking very similar to MEDC cities
2 High-quality housing – expensive apartments and large houses on best quality land, close to CBD and along main roads
3 Medium-quality housing – oldest housing, improved by occupants over several decades
4 Low-quality housing – self-built using bricks and corrugated iron (improved shanty towns)
5 Shanty towns – newest housing on the city outskirts built from scrap wood, metal and plastic
6 Industry – zones of industry have developed along roads and railways

Progress check

1 Describe the Burgess land use model.

2 Describe the Hoyt land use model.

3 Why is land in the CBD the most expensive?

4 What is the inner city?

5 What is a shanty town?

6 Match the descriptions below with the correct urban land use zone.

a) Shops and offices	High-cost housing
b) Abandoned industry and derelict land	CBD
c) Terraced housing and tower blocks	Medium-cost housing
d) Semi-detached housing	Transition zone
e) Detached housing	Low-cost housing

DAY
4

URBANISATION

Urbanisation is the increase in the percentage of people living in towns and cities.

Urbanisation occurred in Western Europe during the Nineteenth Century for one key reason:

- **The Industrial Revolution** – farm labourers migrated from rural areas to towns to find higher-paying jobs working in coal mines or factories, e.g. iron and steel and textiles.

Urbanisation in poorer countries (LEDCs) has been occurring rapidly since the 1950s. This is happening for two main reasons:

- **Rural to urban migration** – caused by a lack of services in the countryside and the prospect of a better future in the city

- **Population growth** – high birth rates

MEDC urban issues

Inner-city areas had deteriorated by the 1960s for a number of reasons.
Example: Manchester, England

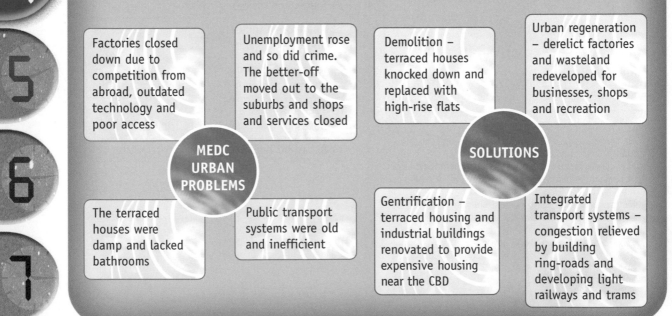

Factories closed down due to competition from abroad, outdated technology and poor access

Unemployment rose and so did crime. The better-off moved out to the suburbs and shops and services closed

Demolition – terraced houses knocked down and replaced with high-rise flats

Urban regeneration – derelict factories and wasteland redeveloped for businesses, shops and recreation

MEDC URBAN PROBLEMS

SOLUTIONS

The terraced houses were damp and lacked bathrooms

Public transport systems were old and inefficient

Gentrification – terraced housing and industrial buildings renovated to provide expensive housing near the CBD

Integrated transport systems – congestion relieved by building ring-roads and developing light railways and trams

LEDC urban issues

The rapid growth of cities in LEDCs has resulted in a number of problems. **Example: Rio de Janeiro, Brazil**

Unemployment – there are not enough jobs for the migrants who arrive in the city

Housing – most migrants build their own shelters from scrap materials on the city outskirts: conditions are very poor with no clean water and no electricity

LEDC URBAN PROBLEMS

Services – there are not enough schools or hospitals to meet the needs of everyone

Transport – congestion jams the streets for hours and the air is thick with exhaust fumes

Investment – transnational companies are encouraged to invest in factories since this provides jobs

Housing – self-help schemes, site and service schemes and the construction of new towns provides more quality housing

SOLUTIONS

Services – government and charities fund schools and clinics in the shanty towns

Transport – congestion is tackled by improving the road networks and improving public transport

Progress check

1 What is urbanisation?

2 Why did urbanisation occur in Western Europe?

3 Why did urbanisation occur in LEDCs?

4 When did urbanisation begin in Western Europe?
a) 1600s
b) 1700s
c) 1800s
d) 1900s

5 When did urbanisation begin in many LEDCs?
a) 1920s
b) 1940s
c) 1950s
d) 1980s

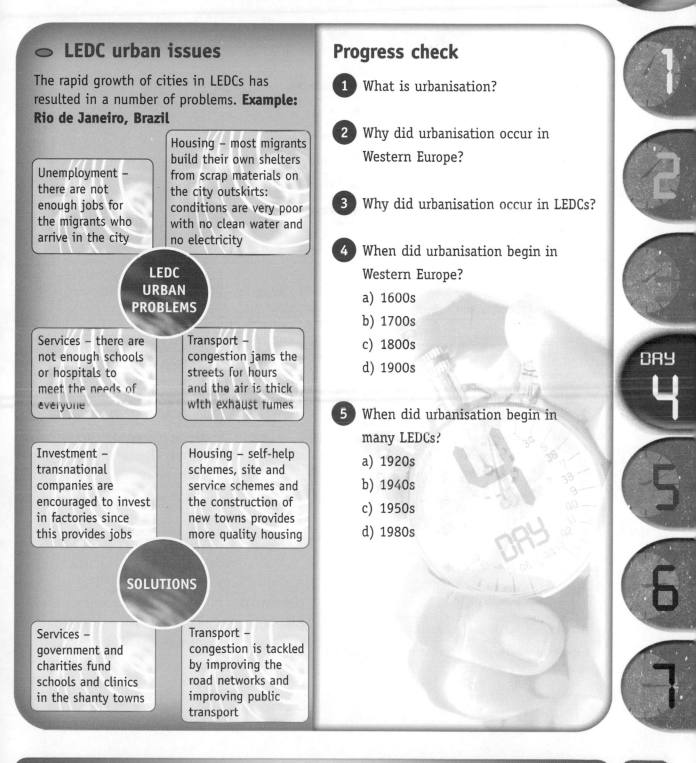

Farming as a system

Inputs	→	Processes	→	Outputs
Climate	→	Ploughing	→	Crops
Labour	→	Harvesting	→	Animals
Relief	→	Planting	→	Animal products
Seeds	→	Grazing	→	Waste
Soil	→	Weeding	→	Profit
Animals	→	Milking		

Relief – flat land is easier to farm as machinery can be used more easily, and there is less soil erosion

Politics – governments control subsidies (money to encourage production) and quotas (limits on production)

Choice – personal interests will affect the farmer's decisions

Climate – crops need between 250mm and 500mm of rainfall a year, and a minimum of 6°C

FACTORS AFFECTING FARMING

Soil – needs to be fertile to grow crops

Finance – farmers need money to buy seeds, chemicals and machinery

Labour – people who work on the farm

Market – demand and price for products

Classification

Arable	Crops such as wheat, barley, maize and potatoes
Pastoral	Farm animals for meat and other animal products
Mixed	Arable and pastoral farming
Intensive	A large investment of money, labour or equipment is used to provide high yields per hectare

Extensive	Relatively low inputs of money, labour or equipment to produce modest yields per hectare
Commercial	Run as a business to produce profit
Subsistence	Aims to produce enough food to support the farmer and his family
Nomadic	Seasonal movements of livestock to fresh pasture, or shifting cultivation
Sedentary	Farming in a fixed location

Farming provides the world's population with most of its food and many other essential products.

Farming in the UK

Dairy farming

Physical factors – flat land; fertile, well-drained soils to grow high-quality grass; mild winters; and regular rainfall

Human factors – good access to urban markets for fresh dairy products

Locations – western parts of England, Scotland and Wales

Arable farming

Physical factors – flat land; deep fertile soils; reliable rain; and warm summers

Human factors – minimum prices are guaranteed for some crops by the EU

Locations – south-east England and east Scotland

Sheep and beef cattle farming

Physical factors – high land; thin, infertile soils; high rainfall; and low temperatures

Human factors – subsidies are provided by the EU for hill farms

Locations – upland areas in England, Wales and Scotland

Market gardening

Physical factors – plenty of sunshine, other factors are controlled in glasshouses

Human factors – large investment of money, food fashions and access to markets

Locations – south-east England, the Fens and Isles of Scilly

Progress check

1. Classify the following as either **physical factors** or **human factors** affecting farming:

   a) Politics   e) Market
   b) Relief   f) Finance
   c) Labour   g) Choice
   d) Soil   h) Climate

2. Which of the locations shown on the map are best suited to the following types of farming?
   Arable
   Dairy
   Sheep and beef
   Market gardening

FARMING IN EUROPE

Common Agricultural Policy

In 1963 the **Common Agricultural Policy** (CAP) was agreed by the UK government and other European countries (now the European Union, EU).

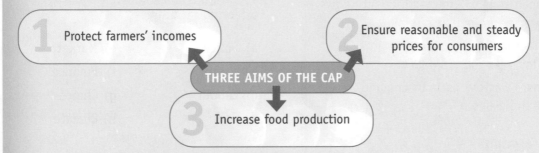

1 Protect farmers' incomes

2 Ensure reasonable and steady prices for consumers

THREE AIMS OF THE CAP

3 Increase food production

The CAP works through two key strategies:

- Subsidies and grants – money is given to farmers who live in remote areas that are difficult to farm profitably, e.g. hill sheep farmers in Wales.

- Price support – a guaranteed minimum price for agricultural produce. Produce is bought and stored by the EU.

Environmental impacts of farming

The CAP has been very effective – in fact, we now have surpluses of many products. However, as farming has intensified it has had a greater impact on the environment.

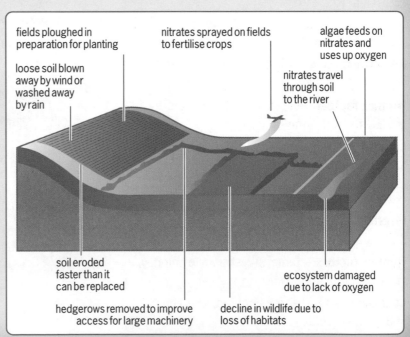

fields ploughed in preparation for planting

nitrates sprayed on fields to fertilise crops

algae feeds on nitrates and uses up oxygen

loose soil blown away by wind or washed away by rain

nitrates travel through soil to the river

soil eroded faster than it can be replaced

ecosystem damaged due to lack of oxygen

hedgerows removed to improve access for large machinery

decline in wildlife due to loss of habitats

DAY 5

Diversification

Farmers have moved into areas other than farming to boost their income. This is known as farm diversification, and includes ideas such as:

- Converting barns into holiday cottages
- Opening tea shops and visitor centres
- Selling produce in farm shops

Genetically modified organisms

GMOs are plants or animals which have had their genes altered to improve them in some way. The potential benefits of GMOs are huge, but many people worry about this new technology.

- Benefits – plants become resistant to diseases, droughts, frost and insects
- Concerns – genes may 'escape' and breed superweeds, and the effects on people's health is not known

Organic farming

Concern over GMOs and problems such as 'mad cow disease' have increased the demand for organic products.

- Crops are grown without artificial chemicals and fertilisers
- Animals are reared without regular injections of antibiotics

Progress check

True or false?

1. CAP stands for Common Agricultural Practice.

2. The CAP aims to protect farmers' incomes.

3. The CAP guarantees a minimum price for agricultural produce.

4. Ploughing fields helps to prevent soil erosion.

5. Fertiliser sprayed on fields can damage ecosystems.

6. The EU pays farmers not to grow anything on some of their land.

7. Farm diversification includes opening tea shops.

8. GMO stands for Genetically Mutated Organism.

9. GMO crops may be drought and frost resistant.

10. Organic farmers use chemical fertilisers to grow healthy crops.

DAY 5

The Green Revolution

Rapid population growth in LEDCs has led to an increased demand for food. During the 1960s and 1970s it was thought that high-technology farming methods were the solution. These methods became known as the **Green Revolution**.

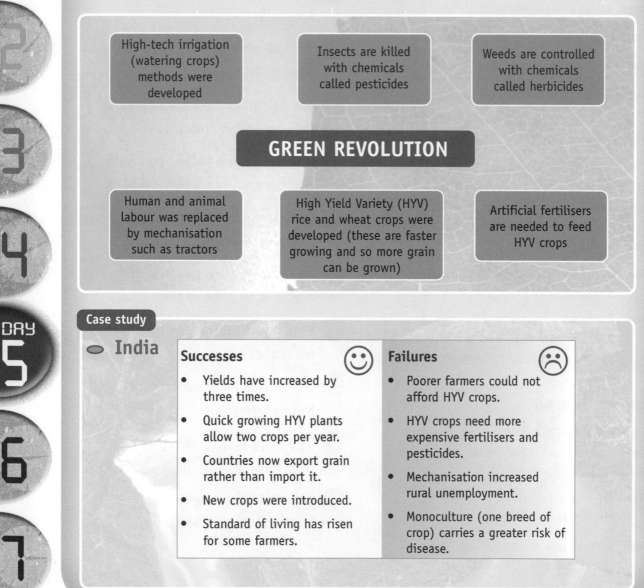

High-tech irrigation (watering crops) methods were developed

Insects are killed with chemicals called pesticides

Weeds are controlled with chemicals called herbicides

GREEN REVOLUTION

Human and animal labour was replaced by mechanisation such as tractors

High Yield Variety (HYV) rice and wheat crops were developed (these are faster growing and so more grain can be grown)

Artificial fertilisers are needed to feed HYV crops

Case study

India

Successes 🙂	Failures ☹
• Yields have increased by three times.	• Poorer farmers could not afford HYV crops.
• Quick growing HYV plants allow two crops per year.	• HYV crops need more expensive fertilisers and pesticides.
• Countries now export grain rather than import it.	• Mechanisation increased rural unemployment.
• New crops were introduced.	• Monoculture (one breed of crop) carries a greater risk of disease.
• Standard of living has risen for some farmers.	

The challenge in poorer countries is to increase food production in an affordable and sustainable way.

10 MINS

Appropriate technology

Although the Green Revolution was successful in a number of ways, it widened the gap between rich and poor farmers. Today, it is realised that food production can also be increased using low-technology methods that can be available to all farmers in poorer countries.

- **Irrigation from local wells and water pumps** can be more effective than large-scale projects such as dams. Drip irrigation provides just enough water for each plant and conserves supplies.

- **Planting trees as windbreaks** is preventing soil from being blown away. In some areas, stones are placed in lines across fields to stop soil from being washed away by rain.

- Planting crops that put **nitrogen** back into the soil (legumes) is restoring soil fertility. This means there is less need for artificial fertilisers.

- **Inter-cropping** increases the amount of food produced by growing plants at different heights on the same piece of land. This can include a combination of root vegetables, low-growing crops and trees.

- Well-designed **grain stores** can significantly reduce the amount of the crop lost to rats, mice, insects and disease. This means less food needs to be grown overall.

DAY 5

Industry as a system

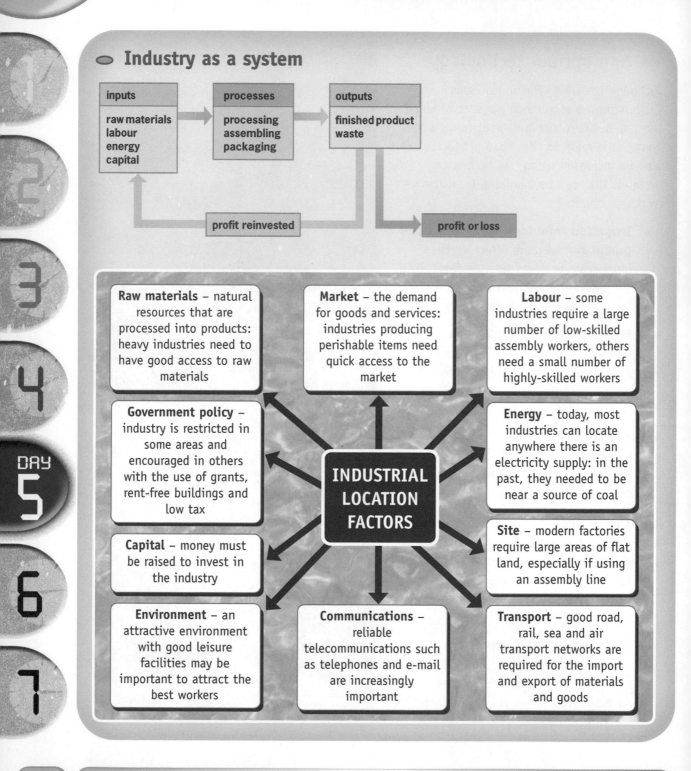

inputs		processes		outputs
raw materials labour energy capital	→	processing assembling packaging	→	finished product waste

profit reinvested

profit or loss

Raw materials – natural resources that are processed into products: heavy industries need to have good access to raw materials

Market – the demand for goods and services: industries producing perishable items need quick access to the market

Labour – some industries require a large number of low-skilled assembly workers, others need a small number of highly-skilled workers

Government policy – industry is restricted in some areas and encouraged in others with the use of grants, rent-free buildings and low tax

INDUSTRIAL LOCATION FACTORS

Energy – today, most industries can locate anywhere there is an electricity supply: in the past, they needed to be near a source of coal

Capital – money must be raised to invest in the industry

Site – modern factories require large areas of flat land, especially if using an assembly line

Environment – an attractive environment with good leisure facilities may be important to attract the best workers

Communications – reliable telecommunications such as telephones and e-mail are increasingly important

Transport – good road, rail, sea and air transport networks are required for the import and export of materials and goods

Industry is any type of economic activity involving the manufacture of goods or the provision of services.

Types of industry

Industry is classified into four types.

Primary industry

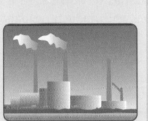

The extraction or production of raw materials. It includes agriculture, forestry, fishing and mining.

Secondary industry

The processing of raw materials, or assembling of parts, to manufacture a finished product. Secondary industry includes steel-making and car assembly.

Tertiary industry

The provision of services such as health, administration, retailing and transport. Tertiary industries are also called service industries.

Quaternary industry

The provision of technical advice, or research and development. It includes work in biotechnology, communications and information technology.

Progress check

1 Match the descriptions below with the correct location factor.

a) Docks for importing and exporting	Transport
b) A skilled workforce	Market
c) Investment to establish industry	Labour
d) Low taxes for the first five years	Government policy
e) Consumers wanting to buy a product	Raw materials
f) Natural resources	Capital

2 Classify the following occupations as **primary, secondary, tertiary** or **quaternary** industry.

a) Software developer
b) Farmer
c) Steel worker
d) Miner
e) Baker
f) Accountant
g) Research chemist
h) Shop assistant

DAY
5

INDUSTRY IN THE UK

Industrial Revolution

Industry developed on a large scale in the UK during the 1800s. This was due to the invention of steam-driven machines (powered by coal). This period, known as the Industrial Revolution, had two key impacts:

- Farm mechanisation took away jobs previously done by people, causing unemployment in the countryside.

- New industries, including iron, steel and textile manufacturing, began in the towns.

The new industries, and coal mines, needed thousands of workers. As a result there was a massive rural to urban migration, and towns with industry expanded into cities.

Location in the UK

The factories and mills were built close to their raw materials, because these were bulky to transport. **Example: steel industry, South Wales**.

Industrial decline

By the 1960s, traditional industries had declined for two key reasons:

Labour costs

Lower wages in foreign countries meant that goods produced by the UK were relatively expensive. Many factories were forced to close because they could no longer compete.

World market

Many of the UK's colonies, such as India, gained their independence. These countries no longer had to buy goods from the UK. Factories in the UK had fewer markets for their goods.

Traditional industries in the UK

Central Scotland – iron, steel, ships cotton goods

North-East England – iron, steel, ships

Lancashire – cotton goods

Yorkshire – woollen goods, cutlery

Northern Ireland – ships, textiles

Derby/ Nottingham – coal mining

West Midlands – cars, metal goods

East Midlands – iron/ steel

South Wales – iron/steel metal working

London – manufactured goods

Heavy industry has come and gone in the UK, replaced by a new generation of footloose businesses.

15 MINS

Modern industries

As heavy industries such as iron and steel have declined, modern industries have taken their place. Modern industries are often described as 'footloose'. This means they have much more choice about where they locate, because they do not use heavy, bulky raw materials. Modern industries have two key location factors:

- **transport** – they need to be close to motorways, railways and airports

- **labour** – assembly industries require a lower skilled, lower paid workforce; high-tech industries need a highly-skilled workforce

Modern industries tend to locate on the edge of urban areas in business parks or industrial estates. **Example: Microsoft, Reading, England**

- **light manufacturing** – small products such as electrical goods or processed food

- **high-technology industry** – high-value electronic goods such as computers and biotechnology

- **administration** – office work, e.g. law, finance, government, telephone call centres

- **leisure industry** – recreation facilities, e.g. cinemas, leisure centres, restaurants

- **retail industry** – shops, retail parks, out of town shopping centres

Progress check

Cross out the incorrect words in the sentences below:

a) The Industrial Revolution began during the **1800s/1900s**.

b) The Industrial Revolution resulted in migration **to/from** the cities.

c) Factories were built close to their **market/raw materials**.

d) The cotton industry was located in **Yorkshire/Lancashire**.

e) Traditional industries declined in the UK in the **1930s/1960s**.

f) The UK **gained/lost** markets when its colonies gained independence.

g) **Modern/heavy** industry is described as footloose.

h) Modern industries prefer to locate near the city **centre/outskirts**.

DAY 5

INDUSTRY IN LEDCs

LEDCs and informal industry

Many of the world's poorest countries did not experience an Industrial Revolution. The majority of people in LEDCs still work in farming. A small percentage of people work in formal industry (employed with fixed hours and wages), while the rest work in the informal sector (self-employed street sellers).

Case study

Kenya

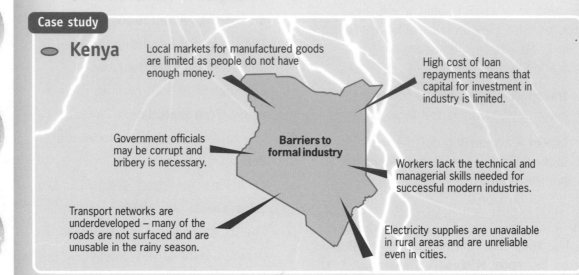

Local markets for manufactured goods are limited as people do not have enough money.

High cost of loan repayments means that capital for investment in industry is limited.

Government officials may be corrupt and bribery is necessary.

Barriers to formal industry

Workers lack the technical and managerial skills needed for successful modern industries.

Transport networks are underdeveloped – many of the roads are not surfaced and are unusable in the rainy season.

Electricity supplies are unavailable in rural areas and are unreliable even in cities.

Environmental impacts

LEDCs are at risk from pollution from industry because many do not have strict environmental laws yet.

Case study

Bhopal, India

In 1984, the Union Carbide factory producing pesticides and fertilisers exploded.

Air	Toxic cloud covered an area 40 km^2 killing 12 000 people and injuring 5000
Land	Soil contaminated with chemicals including nickel and mercury – this transferred to fruits and vegetables, and then people
Water	Water supply for 20 000 people contaminated with chemicals known to cause cancer, liver and kidney damage

DAY 5

Transnational corporations

Transnational corporations (TNCs), or multinationals, are very large companies with offices, factories, mines or plantations in many different countries. **Example: Nike.**

Location

- Headquarters and research and development offices are usually located in MEDCs.
- Factories, mines and plantations are likely to be located in LEDCs where low labour costs increase profits.
- LEDC governments encourage TNCs by offering low taxes.

Advantages of TNCs to LEDCs ☺

- Local people gain employment and a steady income.
- Local businesses benefit from wages spent by workers.
- Taxes are paid to the government by the TNCs and workers.
- Taxes are used to fund schools and hospitals.

Disadvantages of TNCs to LEDCs ☹

- The profit goes to shareholders in MEDCs.
- Many jobs are unskilled and low paid.
- Working conditions can be very tough and dangerous.
- TNCs cause environmental damage and then leave.

Progress check

1. What is meant by the term 'formal industry'?

2. What is meant by the term 'informal industry'?

3. Why is foreign debt a barrier to industrialisation for LEDCs?

4. What is a TNC?

5. Name an example of a TNC.

6. Classify the following as **advantages** or **disadvantages** of TNCs to LEDCs.
   a) Working conditions can be dangerous.
   b) There are more jobs available.
   c) Company shareholders in MEDCs make a profit.
   d) Taxes are used to pay for more teachers and doctors.
   e) Employees may learn new skills.
   f) Jobs are low paid.

1
2
3
4
DAY
5
6
7

TOURISM

Tourism is a visit to a place for recreation involving at least one overnight stay. It is an increasingly important industry that accounts for 8% of world trade.

Tourist destinations

Different environments attract tourists.

Scenery – interesting natural landforms such as mountains, lakes and waterfalls attract tourists who like to 'sightsee', e.g. Norway.

Climate – hot and dry climates are ideal for people who like to relax in the sun. Mountainous areas with reliable snowfall may develop a skiing industry, e.g. Colorado, USA.

Culture – experiencing a different way of life is the key to a good holiday for some people. Culture includes language, music, food, drink and art, e.g. Japan.

Ecology – exotic wildlife, trees and plants are an attraction for some people. Safaris have become popular holidays, e.g. Kenya.

Activities – organised adventure holidays including things such as white water rafting are increasingly popular, e.g. New Zealand.

Impacts of tourism

Positive ☺	Negative ☹
Social – local culture and traditions are saved because they attract tourists.	**Social** – tourists may show a lack of respect for local culture, for example, by getting drunk.
Environmental – money from tourism is used to provide protection for historic buildings and wildlife.	**Environmental** – ecosystems are damaged by building hotels, roads and airports.
Economic – jobs are created, improving standards of living.	**Economic** – traditional jobs are replaced by unreliable, seasonal jobs.

Why is tourism a growth industry?

- **Paid holiday** – as countries become wealthier, companies offer more paid annual leave. The average time off work in Europe is 36 days a year.

- **Wages** – people are able to afford more holidays because their pay has increased faster than inflation, meaning they have more to spend on leisure. The average UK salary is about £450 a week.

- **Attitudes** – an annual holiday is no longer considered a luxury. Many people expect to have at least one holiday a year.

- **Adventure** – people are seeking excitement and adventure on holiday to make a change from the safe lives they live at home.

- **Television** – the number of travel programmes showing sunny places that persuade people to book their next holiday has increased because of satellite and cable television.

- **Air fares** – budget airlines such as easyJet have reduced the cost of travelling abroad.

- **Life expectancy** – people are living longer and retiring earlier, giving them more opportunities to go on holiday.

Progress check

1 Complete the following sentences using the words below:

a) It is predicted there will be ... billion tourist visits a year by 2010.

b) Tourism accounts for ... percent of world trade.

c) The average holiday in Europe is ... days a year.

d) More elderly people are taking holidays because life expectancy is ...

e) More people are taking holidays because air fares are ...

thirty-six	one	eight
decreasing	increasing	

2 Which is the most important factor for the following holidays?

a) Walking in the Yorkshire Dales	Climate
b) Mountain biking in Portugal	Scenery
c) Snow boarding in Japan	Ecology
d) Whale watching in the USA	Culture
e) A weekend in Prague	Activities

Why is the Lake District a popular tourist destination?

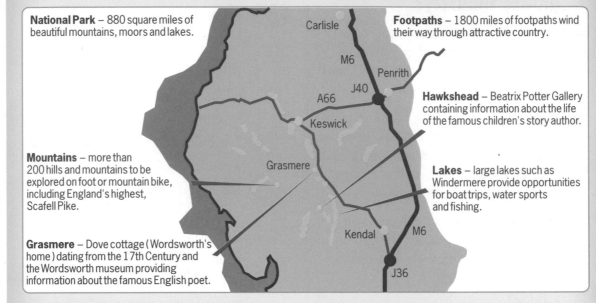

National Park – 880 square miles of beautiful mountains, moors and lakes.

Footpaths – 1800 miles of footpaths wind their way through attractive country.

Hawkshead – Beatrix Potter Gallery containing information about the life of the famous children's story author.

Mountains – more than 200 hills and mountains to be explored on foot or mountain bike, including England's highest, Scafell Pike.

Lakes – large lakes such as Windermere provide opportunities for boat trips, water sports and fishing.

Grasmere – Dove cottage (Wordsworth's home) dating from the 17th Century and the Wordsworth museum providing information about the famous English poet.

Map labels: Carlisle, M6, Penrith, J40, A66, Keswick, Grasmere, Kendal, M6, J36

Impacts of tourism in the Lake District

Positive ☺	Negative ☹
● Tourism has provided employment for local people, for example, working in shops, restaurants, hotels, and providing services such as boat trips.	● Large numbers of cars and coaches on narrow country roads leads to congestion and an increase in air pollution in the towns.
● Demand for housing has pushed up property prices, increasing the wealth of people who already own their own homes.	● The huge numbers of walkers has resulted in footpaths being worn away. During heavy rain this leads to soil erosion and gullying.
● National Park status has ensured that the Lake District is protected from inappropriate development such as large housing estates or industrial buildings.	● Many houses have been bought as holiday homes. Many locals cannot now afford to buy their own homes.
● The Lake District provides opportunities for recreation for millions each year, including locals.	● Areas that attract the most visitors are known as 'honey pots'. The development of honey pots, such as Bowness, is ruining features that made them popular in the first place.

15 MINS

Managing tourism

The National Park Authority, together with local authorities and organisations such as the National Trust, work to minimise the negative impacts of tourism. Tourism has been managed in the following ways:

- **Car parks** have been built on the outskirts of popular towns and people are encouraged to use public transport rather than driving.

- **Footpaths** have been paved and reinforced in the most heavily used areas. The use of local stone means that the footpaths blend with the environment. This has prevented soil erosion and gullying.

- New **housing developments** have been allowed, and a proportion of homes are only available to people who live and work in the area.

- Holiday companies have included an **'optional tax'** of £1 per person on the price of each holiday. This money has been used to restore footpaths and protect wildlife.

- A **speed restriction** of 10 kilometres per hour has been imposed on the 17 000 craft licensed to sail on Lake Windermere.

- Tourism has been deliberately **concentrated** in certain areas such as Ambleside and Keswick in order to protect more fragile areas.

Progress check

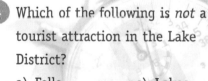

1. Where is the Lake District?

2. How many tourists visit the Lake District each year?
   a) 6 million   c) 10 million
   b) 8 million   d) 12 million

3. Which of the following is a positive impact of tourism in the Lake District?
   a) Congestion on the roads
   b) Increase in property prices
   c) Footpath erosion
   d) Overcrowding of popular locations

4. Which of the following is *not* a tourist attraction in the Lake District?
   a) Fells   c) Lakes
   b) Fjords   d) Moors

5. Which of the following has *not* been used to manage tourism in the Lake District?
   a) Entry fee
   b) Footpath construction
   c) Tax on holidays
   d) Improved public transport

DAY 6

TOURISM IN KENYA

Why is Kenya a popular tourist destination?

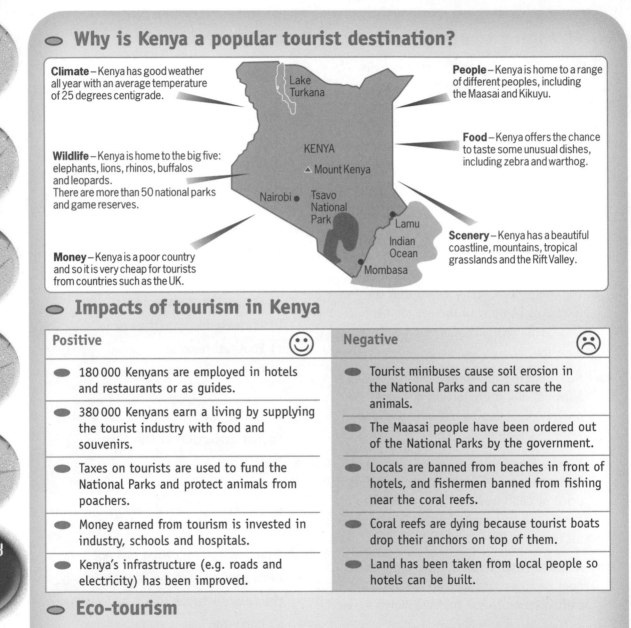

Climate – Kenya has good weather all year with an average temperature of 25 degrees centigrade.

Wildlife – Kenya is home to the big five: elephants, lions, rhinos, buffalos and leopards.
There are more than 50 national parks and game reserves.

Money – Kenya is a poor country and so it is very cheap for tourists from countries such as the UK.

People – Kenya is home to a range of different peoples, including the Maasai and Kikuyu.

Food – Kenya offers the chance to taste some unusual dishes, including zebra and warthog.

Scenery – Kenya has a beautiful coastline, mountains, tropical grasslands and the Rift Valley.

Lake Turkana · KENYA · Mount Kenya · Nairobi · Tsavo National Park · Lamu · Indian Ocean · Mombasa

Impacts of tourism in Kenya

Positive 😊	Negative ☹
180 000 Kenyans are employed in hotels and restaurants or as guides.	Tourist minibuses cause soil erosion in the National Parks and can scare the animals.
380 000 Kenyans earn a living by supplying the tourist industry with food and souvenirs.	The Maasai people have been ordered out of the National Parks by the government.
Taxes on tourists are used to fund the National Parks and protect animals from poachers.	Locals are banned from beaches in front of hotels, and fishermen banned from fishing near the coral reefs.
Money earned from tourism is invested in industry, schools and hospitals.	Coral reefs are dying because tourist boats drop their anchors on top of them.
Kenya's infrastructure (e.g. roads and electricity) has been improved.	Land has been taken from local people so hotels can be built.

Eco-tourism

In some places in Kenya, mass tourism has damaged the environment and had negative effects on the local people. In a number of areas, eco-tourism (sustainable tourism) is now being encouraged. Eco-tourism is a type of holiday that minimises impacts on the environment and can provide benefits to the area.

DAY 6

Kenya is a Less Economically Developed Country (LEDC) in East Africa. Mass tourism developed in Kenya in the 1990s.

Case study

◯ Lamu

Lamu is a town located on an island off Kenya's coast. It contains many historical sites and ancient buildings.

Eco-tourism is being developed in Lamu in the following ways:

- Lamu is a traditional Islamic community, and women still wear veils in public. Tourists in swimming trunks and bikinis can cause great offence, especially if they wander into town in their beach wear. Large signs have been displayed to encourage tourists to respect local customs.

- Tourists are encouraged to stay in bed and breakfast accommodation in the old town to reduce the need for large new hotels. Any new hotels built must be lower than the height of the palm trees, so they can not be seen from boats out at sea.

- Lamu's oldest buildings are made from coral and mortar, and are plastered on the inside. Tourists staying in Lamu pay a tax that is used to pay for the restoration of historic buildings using traditional building methods.

10 MINS

Classifying resources

Resources can be classified as either **renewable** (should last forever) or **non-renewable** (will eventually run-out).

Non-renewable
- Coal
- Oil
- Gas
- Minerals

RESOURCES

Resources
- Water
- Timber
- Soil
- Fish

Resource depletion

The Earth's resources are being depleted (running out), either because they are finite, or because they are being used up faster than they can be replaced. This is happening for two key reasons:

Population growth
- The global population is more than 6 billion and is expected to increase to 9 billion by 2050.
- The more people there are, the faster resources will be used up.

Development
- The majority of the world's population lives in LEDCs.
- As LEDCs develop economically the demand for goods will increase. This will increase the pressure on resources.

Sustainability

Sustainable development is the concept of meeting the needs of people today without compromising the ability of future generations to meet their needs. Governments of 153 countries agreed a policy of sustainable development at the Earth Summit in Rio, Brazil, in 1992.

- Conserve resources by reducing demand and recycling waste products.
- Encourage family planning to slow population growth.
- Protect habitats, plants and animals.

Resources are parts of the environment used by people to live. Some of the Earth's resources are being used up at an alarming rate.

Waste

Waste is material that may no longer be useful to people.

- The UK average is 350 kilos of waste per person every year.

- Most of our waste (83%) is buried in large landfill sites.

- Landfill sites attract vermin, look unattractive and may leak dangerous chemicals.

- A small amount of waste (9%) is incinerated, which may release dangerous chemicals into the air when plastic is burned.

Recycling

Recycling is when things that have been used once are used again.

- LEDCs recycle much more of their waste than MEDCs.

- It should be possible to recycle about 70% of waste.

- The UK recycles only 8% of its waste.

- Recycling saves resources and energy, as well as reducing pollution.

Progress check

True or false?

1. Fish are a renewable resource.

2. Timber is a renewable resource.

3. Gas is a renewable resource.

4. The Earth's resources are being depleted because of population growth.

5. As countries become more developed they use fewer resources.

6. Sustainability is the concept of using what we need today without considering the future.

7. 153 countries agreed a policy of sustainable development in Rio in 1992.

8. The average person in the UK produces 350 kilos of waste a year.

9. It is possible to recycle 99% of waste.

10. The UK recycles 8% of its waste.

DAY
6

ENERGY

Energy is the power needed to run machines and provide heat and light.

Sources of energy can be divided into non-renewable and renewable resources.

Non-renewable energy

Coal, oil and gas are non-renewable **fossil fuels**. They are called 'fossil fuels' because they have formed over millions of years from the remains of plants and animals.

Coal – formed from the remains of trees and plants that died 300 million years ago.

Advantages – efficient source of energy with known reserves that will last for 300 years.

Disadvantages – gases produced by burning coal add to global warming and acid rain.

Oil and gas – formed from the remains of tiny sea creatures that died 200 million years ago.

Advantages – less polluting than coal and easy to transport by pipeline or tanker.

Disadvantages – limited reserves (oil 45 years, gas 70 years). Oil spills damage ecosystems.

Energy consumption

Global energy consumption is increasing every year, for two key reasons:

- Population growth – the more people there are, the more energy will be needed.

- Economic development – the richer people become, the more things they can buy that need energy.

Renewable energy

Renewable energy resources should last forever. These include hydroelectric power (HEP), solar, wind, geothermal, wave and tidal power.

Wind power

Wind turbines are an increasingly popular source of renewable energy. Large rotor blades are angled to face the wind and are turned at up to 400 km per hour. A generator converts the wind energy into electricity.

Wind turbines are usually located in upland regions with reliable strong winds, particularly in areas a long way from the main electricity grid. However, recently the UK government has encouraged the development of 'offshore wind farms' – large banks of turbines built out to sea.

Advantages	Disadvantages
Relatively cheap source of electricity that does not produce greenhouse gases	Wind turbines can look very out of place in areas of natural beauty
An adaptable form of energy that can provide energy for a single house or contribute to the national grid	Rotor blades are noisy and may affect wildlife, such as birds

Progress check

1. Classify the following as **non-renewable** or **renewable** energy resources
   a) Solar
   b) Coal
   c) Oil
   d) Wave
   e) Gas
   f) Wind

2. Cross out the incorrect words in the sentences below:

   a) Coal is formed from trees and plants that died **200/300** million years ago.
   b) Oil is **easy/difficult** to transport by pipeline.
   c) Global energy consumption is **increasing/decreasing**
   d) Wind turbines **do/do not** produce greenhouse gases.

DEVELOPMENT

What is development?

Development is the use of resources and technology to increase wealth and improve quality of life. Four kinds of development are:

- **economic development** – increase in income and wealth due to growth of industry

- **environmental development** – improving or restoring the natural environment

- **social development** – improvements in standards of living through education and healthcare

- **political development** – progression to democracy and free elections

Contrasts in development

Not all countries have developed at the same rate and globally there is a very unequal distribution of wealth.

MEDCs have 20% of the world's population.

MEDCs own 80% of the world's wealth.

The richer countries are known as More Economically Developed Countries (MEDCs).

MEDCs are mainly in the northern hemisphere – USA, Canada, Western Europe and Japan (exceptions Australia and New Zealand).

☐ MEDCs   ■ LEDCs

The poorer countries are known as Less Economically Developed Countries (LEDCs).

LEDCs are mainly in the southern hemisphere – continents of South America, Africa and Asia.

Why are countries underdeveloped?

less economically developed country

not enough money to invest in industries, schools and hospitals

lack of industry, poor education and healthcare

few manufactured exports, many people cannot read and write, illness

The world is an unequal place. There are relatively few rich people. The majority are poor.

15 MINS

How is development measured?

Economic development is measured using **Gross National Product (GNP)** per capita.

- GNP per capita is the total value of all goods and services produced by a country in one year, divided by the total population to give an average per person.

Social development is measured using data about people.

- **birth rate** – number of live births per thousand people per year
- **death rate** – number of deaths per thousand people per year
- **infant mortality** – number of infant deaths per thousand live births per year
- **life expectancy** – average life span
- **population per doctor** – the number of people to one doctor

The Human Development Index (HDI) was created by the United Nations and combines economic and social data to give a more balanced picture of development:

- **income per person** – adjusted for the cost of living in that country
- **education** – percentage of adults who are literate, and average number of years in education
- **life expectancy**

Progress check

1. What is meant by the term 'development'?

2. What do the letters MEDC stand for?

3. What do the letters LEDC stand for?

4. What percentage of the world's population live in MEDCs?

5. What percentage of the world's wealth is owned by people living in MEDCs?

6. In which hemisphere are most LEDCs found?

7. What is meant by the term 'Gross National Product'?

8. What is meant by the term 'birth rate'?

9. What do the letters HDI stand for?

10. How does the HDI give a balanced picture of development?

DAY 6

7

TRADE

What is trade?

International trade is the exchange of goods and services between countries. Trade usually happens when a producing country is able to produce goods or services more cheaply, or of better quality, than the consuming country.

- Imports are goods bought by a country from another country.

- Exports are goods sold by a country to another country.

- Balance of trade is the difference between the value of the imports and exports.

Pattern of international trade

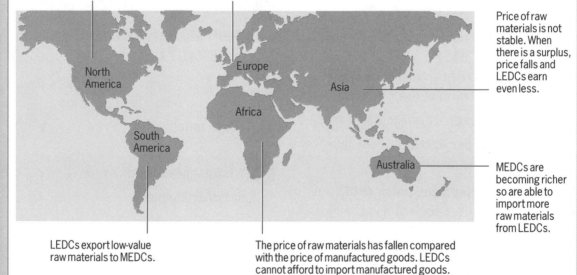

MEDCs export high-value manufactured and processed goods to LEDCs.

The price of manufactured goods increases steadily every year.

Price of raw materials is not stable. When there is a surplus, price falls and LEDCs earn even less.

North America

Europe

Asia

Africa

South America

Australia

MEDCs are becoming richer so are able to import more raw materials from LEDCs.

LEDCs export low-value raw materials to MEDCs.

The price of raw materials has fallen compared with the price of manufactured goods. LEDCs cannot afford to import manufactured goods.

This unequal pattern of international trade was established during the Eighteenth and Nineteenth Centuries. European countries colonised parts of the Americas, Africa and Asia and imported their resources, such as crops, timber and minerals. The Europeans then exported manufactured goods back to their colonies, e.g. fabric and steam trains to India. Although the colonies are now independent, many are still finding it difficult to break this pattern of trade.

⊙ Fair trade

One way of helping LEDCs to make more money from their exports is through fair trade. Fair trade is a system where the producers of the raw materials for a product are given a fair price. They are also given **long-term contracts**, **health and safety guarantees** and extra **help with education and housing**. This is paid for by making the finished product a little more expensive.

Fair trade usually works on a small scale with individual farmers or a co-operative. However, it also removes some of the problems of trading primary products, which ultimately helps the country as a whole. The most common fair trade products are **tea, coffee, chocolate and fruit.**

At the moment, consumers in MEDCs are still not buying enough fair trade products to make a difference to more than a fraction of the producers in LEDCs. Nevertheless, the situation is improving, due to increased awareness of fair trade products through charities such as Oxfam, Traidcraft and Comic Relief.

A common fair trade product

Progress check

1. What is meant by the word 'trade'?

2. What is meant by the word 'import'?

3. What is meant by the word 'export'?

4. What is meant by the term 'balance of trade'?

5. Fill in the gaps in the sentences below with either the word 'MEDCs' or 'LEDCs'.
   a) ... are becoming relatively poorer.
   b) ... export high value manufactured goods.
   c) ... are becoming richer.
   d) ... export low value primary products.
   e) Fair trade helps farmers in ...
   f) Consumers in ... only buy a small amount of fair trade produce.

DAY 6

Aid

Aid is a transfer of resources from one country to another, usually from an MEDC to an LEDC. Aid can include money, equipment, food, training, skilled people and loans.

Donors and receivers

The United Nations recommends that countries spend 0.7% of their GNP on Overseas Development Aid (ODA) per year.

- Largest donors of aid are Norway, Denmark and Sweden.
- Largest receivers of aid are China, Egypt and Indonesia.

Types of aid

Multilateral aid – arranged by international organisations such as the International Monetary Fund (IMF), United Nations (UN) and the World Bank

Multilateral aid – arranged by international organisations such as the International Monetary Fund (IMF), United Nations (UN) and the World Bank

Emergency aid – short-term immediate relief during or after a disaster, e.g. famine or earthquake: includes blankets, tents, medicine, food, clothes, water and equipment

Long-term aid – aims to increase development and improve standard of living: includes education, training, technology and improvements to infrastructure

Sewage contaminates water supply spreading diseases

Crops ruined and soil saturated, preventing new planting

Bilateral aid – aid from one country to another that is arranged by their own governments

Tied aid – the country that is receiving the aid must agree to spend the money on goods or services from donor country

NGO aid – Non-Governmental Organisations are charities such as Oxfam, which run aid projects: money is raised through private donations but also through government grants

Advantages of aid

- Aid can benefit people in both MEDCs and LEDCs.
- Emergency aid following a natural disaster saves lives.
- Long-term aid such as education can improve the standard of living of people in LEDCs.
- Tied aid boosts exports and secures jobs in MEDCs, e.g. manufacturers of agricultural equipment, such as tractors, may benefit from orders placed by LEDCs.

Disdvantages of aid

- Aid is frequently a loan, with interest to pay, and LEDCs sink further into debt as they have to borrow more to make the payments.
- Food aid may cause local prices to fall and put farmers and shopkeepers in the LEDCs out of business.
- Tied aid may force LEDCs to buy inappropriate technology, e.g. combine harvesters, which are expensive to maintain and cause rural unemployment.
- Large scale infrastructure projects, such as dams and airports, can damage the environment and increase the national debt.

Progress check

1 What is aid?

2 How much does the UN recommend countries spend on aid?

3 Which three countries donate the most aid?

4 Which three countries receive the most aid?

5 Match the descriptions below with the correct type of international aid.

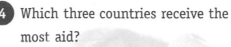

a)	Oxfam provides water pumps for a village in Bangladesh.	Emergency aid
b)	A 50 million dollar donation from the USA to North Korea.	Long term aid
c)	Food air drops in Papua New Guinea following a tidal wave.	Multilateral aid
d)	A 100 million dollar loan to Chad from the World Bank	Bilateral aid
e)	Teachers from Australia spend a year teaching in Vietnam.	Tied aid
f)	Malaysia contracts a UK company to build a dam, using money donated by the UK government.	NGO aid

DAY
7

ECOSYSTEMS

● What is an ecosystem?

An **ecosystem** is a collection of animals, insects, trees and plants living in a certain environment. The living organisms (biomass) in an ecosystem are linked together through food chains, and are dependent on the land, water and air for their survival.

● Global distribution of ecosystems

The type of ecosystem that develops in an area depends mainly on climate.

- **Tropical rainforest** – hundreds of different species of tree: some trees are over 50 metres tall.

- **Deciduous woodland** – trees that shed their leaves in winter, such as oak and ash; shrubs and short grasses.

- **Tropical grassland** – drought resistant trees with waxy leaves and thorns; grasses up to 5 metres tall.

- **Desert** – drought resistant plants, such as cacti, with very long roots to reach deep water supplies.

- **Coniferous forest** – dense evergreen trees, such as fir and pine; few other species.

- **Tundra** – short plants, such as moss, heather and lichen; some stunted trees.

☐ tundra   ■ coniferous forest   ■ temperate grassland   ☐ deciduous woodland   ☐ Mediterranean

☐ ice cap and mountain   ■ tropical rainforest   ☐ tropical grassland   ■ deserts

- **Mediterranean** – evergreen woodland, such as cork and pine; thorny shrubs with thin waxy leaves.

- **Temperate grassland** – grasses up to 2 metres tall; some trees, such as willow.

Coniferous forests

Location

- Areas include northern Europe to Siberia, USA and Canada.

Climate

- Long winters with average monthly temperatures of -30°C.

- Low precipitation because the cold dry air is unable to hold much moisture – total 300mm per year.

- Short summers with long days – average monthly temperatures about 10°C.

Vegetation

Coniferous trees such as spruce, fir and pine. There are few other species at ground level because there is a lack of light and a thick layer of pine needles.

Coniferous trees have adapted to their environment in a number of ways:

- Trees are evergreen so they can grow straight away in spring.

- Conical tree shape allows snow to slide off easily.

- Leaves are needle shaped and waxy to reduce moisture loss.

- Seeds are protected in cones.

Progress check

1 What is meant by the term 'ecosystem'?

2 How are organisms in ecosystems linked together?

3 Where are coniferous forest ecosystems found?

4 Match the descriptions below with the correct ecosystem.

a)	Dense evergreen trees with few other species.	Tropical grassland
b)	Drought resistant trees with waxy leaves.	Desert
c)	Cacti with long roots to reach water.	Coniferous
d)	Oak and ash trees, which lose their leaves in winter.	Tundra
e)	Stunted trees, moss, heather and lichen.	Deciduous woodland

Tropical rainforests

Location

- Tropical rainforests are located between 5° north and south of the equator.
- Areas include Brazil, West Africa and Southeast Asia.

Climate

- High temperatures all year – average 27°C.
- Daily convectional rainfall, totalling over 2000 mm per year.

Soil

- Red clay soils up to 30 metres deep due to rapid weathering.
- Thick leaf litter layer, which decays rapidly due to hot humid climate.
- Soil is leached – nutrients washed out by rain.

Vegetation

Tropical rainforest is stratified into five different layers.

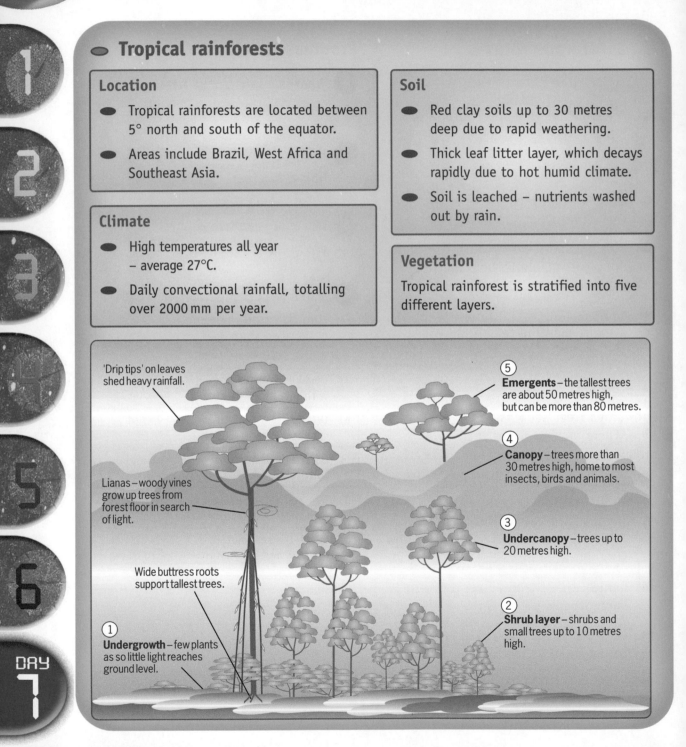

'Drip tips' on leaves shed heavy rainfall.

Lianas – woody vines grow up trees from forest floor in search of light.

Wide buttress roots support tallest trees.

① **Undergrowth** – few plants as so little light reaches ground level.

② **Shrub layer** – shrubs and small trees up to 10 metres high.

③ **Undercanopy** – trees up to 20 metres high.

④ **Canopy** – trees more than 30 metres high, home to most insects, birds and animals.

⑤ **Emergents** – the tallest trees are about 50 metres high, but can be more than 80 metres.

Deforestation

Causes

Agriculture – farmland needed for settlers

Settlement – land needed to provide homes

Ranching – forest cleared to graze cattle

Logging – timber exported, mainly to MEDCs

Mining – gold, iron ore and aluminium ore

Dams – hydro-electric power

Roads – 12 000 km of new roads

Effects

Extinction – rainforests contain 90% of all known species of plants and animals. It is predicted that 100 000 species will become extinct over the next 40 years

Soil erosion – without trees to intercept heavy rainfall, soil is washed into rivers and deforested areas quickly become infertile

Conservation

Sustainable logging – remove only a limited amount of timber each year

Selective felling – remove only most valuable trees such as mahogany

Transport – remove felled trees by helicopter so no new roads are needed

Harvesting – harvest valuable products such as fruit and nuts

Forest Stewardship Council – only buy timber approved by the FSC

Progress check

1. Name an area of rainforest.

2. Give two reasons for deforestation.

3. Describe two impacts of deforestation

4. How can tropical rainforests be managed sustainably?

5. Complete the following sentences using the words below:

   a) Tropical rainforests are located between ... degrees north and south of the equator.

   b) The average temperature in tropical rainforests is ... degrees centigrade.

   c) The average precipitation in a tropical rainforest is over ... millimetres per year.

   d) The tallest trees, emergents, can be over ... metres tall.

   e) The red clay soils found in a tropical rainforest are up to ... metres deep.

   | five | twenty-seven | two-thousand |
   | | eighty | thirty |

Global warming is a rise in the Earths's average temperature caused by an increase in the greenhouse effect.

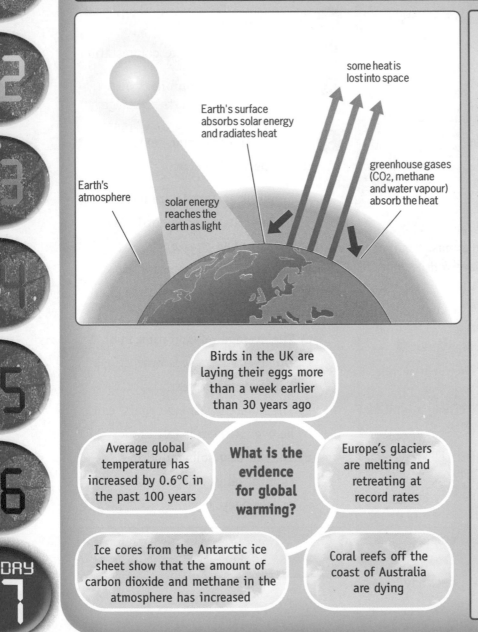

Earth's atmosphere

solar energy reaches the earth as light

Earth's surface absorbs solar energy and radiates heat

some heat is lost into space

greenhouse gases (CO_2, methane and water vapour) absorb the heat

What is the evidence for global warming?

Birds in the UK are laying their eggs more than a week earlier than 30 years ago

Average global temperature has increased by 0.6°C in the past 100 years

Europe's glaciers are melting and retreating at record rates

Ice cores from the Antarctic ice sheet show that the amount of carbon dioxide and methane in the atmosphere has increased

Coral reefs off the coast of Australia are dying

What causes global warming?

It is thought that global warming is happening because people are releasing more greenhouse gases into the atmosphere.

Fossil fuels – coal, oil and gas are burned to provide energy. Burning fossils fuels releases 5000 million tonnes of CO_2 into the atmosphere each year.

Methane – bacteria in flooded rice fields, rotting waste in rubbish dumps and millions of cattle are producing methane gas.

Deforestation – the world's forests are being cut down at an increasing rate. There will be fewer trees converting CO_2 into oxygen.

Global warming is an increase in the Earth's average temperature. It will affect the lives of millions of people worldwide.

What are the possible effects of global warming?

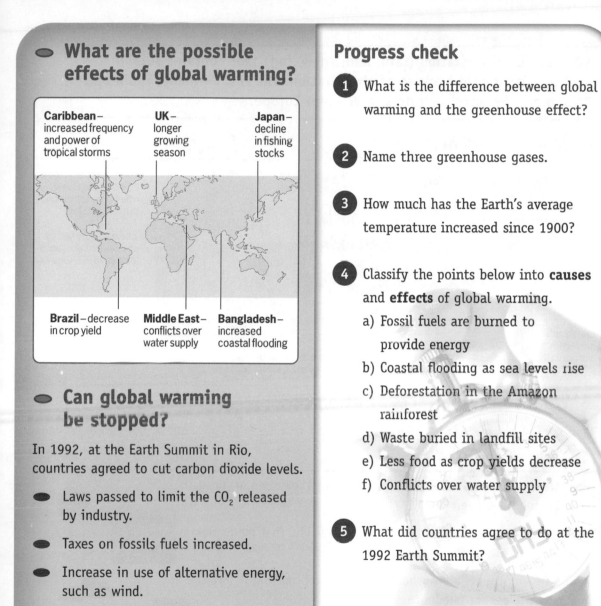

Caribbean – increased frequency and power of tropical storms

UK – longer growing season

Japan – decline in fishing stocks

Brazil – decrease in crop yield

Middle East – conflicts over water supply

Bangladesh – increased coastal flooding

Can global warming be stopped?

In 1992, at the Earth Summit in Rio, countries agreed to cut carbon dioxide levels.

- Laws passed to limit the CO_2 released by industry.

- Taxes on fossils fuels increased.

- Increase in use of alternative energy, such as wind.

Progress check

1. What is the difference between global warming and the greenhouse effect?

2. Name three greenhouse gases.

3. How much has the Earth's average temperature increased since 1900?

4. Classify the points below into **causes** and **effects** of global warming.
   a) Fossil fuels are burned to provide energy
   b) Coastal flooding as sea levels rise
   c) Deforestation in the Amazon rainforest
   d) Waste buried in landfill sites
   e) Less food as crop yields decrease
   f) Conflicts over water supply

5. What did countries agree to do at the 1992 Earth Summit?

DAY 7

ACID RAIN

Acid rain is precipitation (rain, hail, snow, fog) that contains sulphuric acid and nitric acid because of air pollution. The UK, Germany, Spain and Poland are the worst polluters in Western Europe.

What causes acid rain?

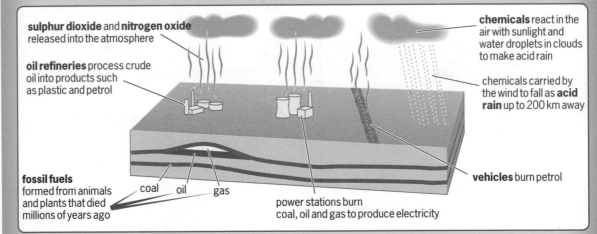

sulphur dioxide and **nitrogen oxide** released into the atmosphere

oil refineries process crude oil into products such as plastic and petrol

fossil fuels formed from animals and plants that died millions of years ago

coal   oil   gas

power stations burn coal, oil and gas to produce electricity

chemicals react in the air with sunlight and water droplets in clouds to make acid rain

chemicals carried by the wind to fall as **acid rain** up to 200 km away

vehicles burn petrol

What are the effects of acid rain?

Clean rainfall has a pH of between 5 and 6. Acid rain has a pH of about 4, but can be as low as 2.4 – the same as vinegar!

- **Trees** – hundreds of thousands of square kilometres of forest in Europe have been killed.

- **Lakes** – 18 000 lakes in Sweden are so acidic that many plants and aquatic life have died.

- **Soil** – nutrients are washed out of the soil, making it infertile and useless for farming.

- **Water supplies** – acid rain releases aluminium, which is harmful to people, into groundwater.

- **Buildings** – rocks such as marble and limestone are worn away by acid rain. The Taj Mahal in India is slowly being dissolved.

Acid rain is an environmental problem affecting mainly industrialised countries.

Solutions?

Countries affected by acid rain have tried to solve the problem in a number of ways.

- Power station and factory chimneys have been made higher so the pollutants are carried further away by the wind. However, this has only made the problem worse elsewhere – 90% of the acid rain falling in Norway comes from other countries.

- Filter systems can be added to power station chimneys. Water and powdered limestone is sprayed through the smoke to neutralise the acid. However, this increases the cost of electricity.

- Catalytic converters have been made compulsory for all new cars in Europe, reducing emissions of nitrogen oxide.

- Alkaline limestone has been added to lakes in Scandinavia to neutralise the acid.

Although the above strategies have helped, the key to reducing acid rain is burning fewer fossil fuels. This can only be achieved by energy conservation, and by developing alternative eco-friendly energy sources such as wind power.

MAP SKILLS

⬭ Relief

Relief, the shape of the land, is shown on Ordnance Survey maps with contour lines, spot heights and triangulation points.

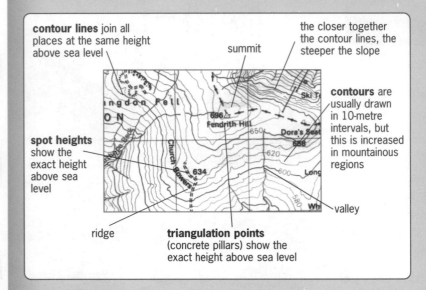

contour lines join all places at the same height above sea level

summit

the closer together the contour lines, the steeper the slope

contours are usually drawn in 10-metre intervals, but this is increased in mountainous regions

spot heights show the exact height above sea level

ridge

triangulation points (concrete pillars) show the exact height above sea level

valley

Useful words for describing relief	
Steep	Gentle
Hilly	Flat
Valley	Ridge

⬭ Distance

The easiest way to measure the distance between two places is with a piece of paper (use the edge of your exam paper if you need to).

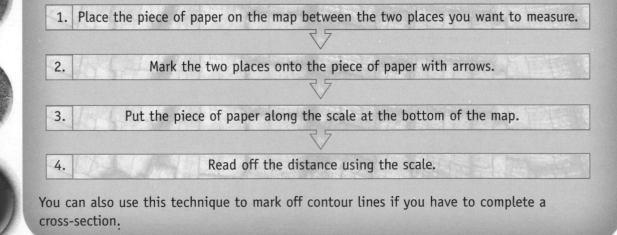

1.	Place the piece of paper on the map between the two places you want to measure.
2.	Mark the two places onto the piece of paper with arrows.
3.	Put the piece of paper along the scale at the bottom of the map.
4.	Read off the distance using the scale.

You can also use this technique to mark off contour lines if you have to complete a cross-section.

Map reading is an essential skill for any Geography exam.

Six-figure grid references

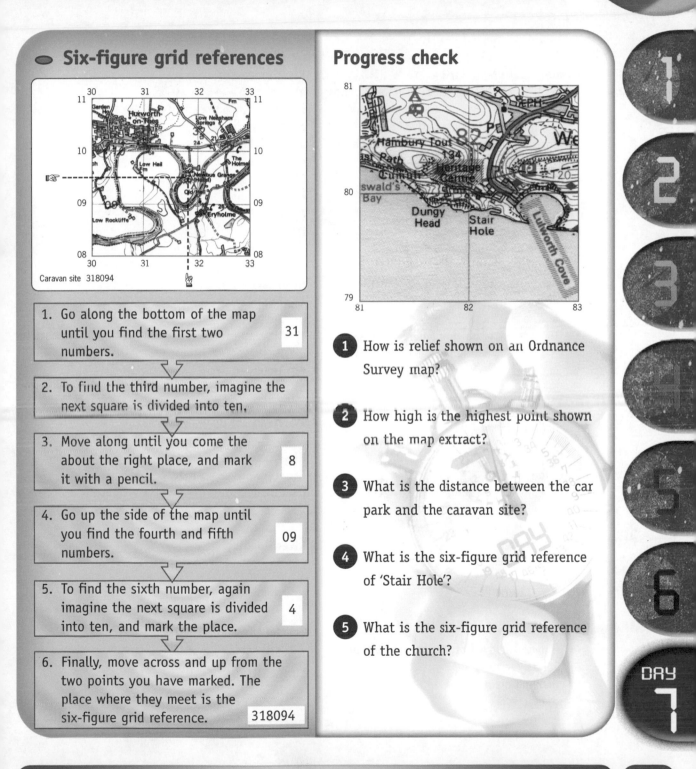

Caravan site 318094

1. Go along the bottom of the map until you find the first two numbers. **31**

2. To find the third number, imagine the next square is divided into ten.

3. Move along until you come the about the right place, and mark it with a pencil. **8**

4. Go up the side of the map until you find the fourth and fifth numbers. **09**

5. To find the sixth number, again imagine the next square is divided into ten, and mark the place. **4**

6. Finally, move across and up from the two points you have marked. The place where they meet is the six-figure grid reference. **318094**

Progress check

1. How is relief shown on an Ordnance Survey map?

2. How high is the highest point shown on the map extract?

3. What is the distance between the car park and the caravan site?

4. What is the six-figure grid reference of 'Stair Hole'?

5. What is the six-figure grid reference of the church?

ANSWERS

Tectonic plate boundaries

1 A place where two or more tectonic plates meet
2 Constructive and destructive
3 Correct words: a = apart, b = destroyed, c = continental, d = conservative
4 a = Iceland, b = Chile, c = Himalayas, d = California

Earthquakes

1 Focus = place underground where earthquake begins
Epicentre = place on surface directly above focus
2 b, d, e, c, f, a
3 India is on a collision boundary between the Indian Plate and the Eurasian Plate.
4 Japan is on a destructive boundary between the Philippine Plate and the Eurasian Plate.
5 Gujurat resulted in a high human cost; Kobe resulted in a high economic cost.

Volcanoes

1 a = Shield, b = Composite, c = Acid, d = Caldera
2 a = Lava flow, b = Pyroclastic flow, c = Ash fall, d = Mudflow

Rocks

1 Igneous
2 Sedimentary
3 Permeable = water can pass through
Impermeable = water cannot pass through
4 Joint = vertical
Bedding plane = horizontal
5 d, c, a, e, b

River processes

a) Solution
b) Hydraulic power
c) Suspension
d) Abrasion
e) Traction
f) Deposition
g) Corrosion
h) Attrition
i) Saltation
j) Erosion

River landforms 1

1 False
2 True
3 True
4 False
5 True
6 False
7 False
8 True

River landforms 2

Correct words: a = erode, b = downstream, c = distributaries, d = loses, e = lightest, f = erode, g = fastest, h = lower

River flooding

1 b
2 b
3 a

Coastal landforms 1

1 b, d, c, e, a
2 a = The Foreland, b = Tilly Whim, c = No Man's Land, d = Old Harry, e = Old Harry's Wife

Coastal landforms 2

1 A collection of sand, pebbles and cobbles on a wave-cut-platform
2 Cliffs, shingle banks, rivers
3 A curved beach sticking into the sea
4 Longshore drift
5 Longshore drift sometimes happens in the opposite direction
6 e, c, d, a, b

Coastal management

1 Local authorities
2 Global warming
3 Yorkshire, Holderness coastline
4 £2.1 million
5 Cliffs to south eroded
6 a = Rock armour, b = Groyne, c = Beach nourishment, d = Cliff stabilisation, e = Managed retreat

Glaciation

1 A river of ice
2 Snowfall exceeds melting
3 Melting exceeds snowfall
4 Slippage, deformation, melting
5 Freeze–thaw, plucking, abrasion
6 a = Five, b = Eighty, c = Thirty, d = Ten, e = Two

Glacial landforms 1

1 A corrie is a deep, circular hollow found near the top of a mountain.
2 Red Tarn, Lake District
3 A tarn is a lake formed in a corrie after the glacier has melted.
4 An arête is a steep-sided ridge found between two corries.
5 Striding Edge, Lake District
6 A pyramidal peak is a sharp, pointed mountain summit.
7 Mount Everest, Nepal
8 Freeze–thaw weathering, plucking and abrasion

Weather

1 True
2 False
3 False
4 True
5 True
6 False
7 True
8 True
9 False
10 False

Climate

1 The average weather
2 a = Hot desert, b = Tropical equatorial, c = Tundra, d = Tropical grassland, e = Temperate maritime, f = Continental interior, g = Mediterranean

Tropical storms

a) Twenty seven
b) Seventy four
c) Five hundred
d) Two
e) One hundred and eighty
f) Eleven thousand
g) Three million
h) Five

Migration

1   a = Push, b = Push, c = Pull, d = Push,
    e = Pull
2   a = False, b = True, c = True, d = True,
    e = False

Settlement

1   Site is the exact location of a settlement.
2   Situation is the location of a settlement
    in relation to the surrounding area.
3   Site = b, c, e, f, h
    Situation = a, d, g

Urban land use models

1   City grows outwards from the centre in a
    series of rings
2   City grows outwards from centre in rings
    and sectors
3   It is the most accessible.
4   The CBD and transition zone
5   Low-quality housing built from scrap
    wood, metal and plastic
6   a = CBD, b = Transition zone, c = Low-
    cost housing, d = Medium-cost housing,
    e = High-cost housing

Urbanisation

1   Increase in the percentage of people
    living in towns and cities
2   Industrial Revolution
3   Rural–urban migration, population growth
4   1800s
5   1950s

Agriculture

1   Physical = b, d, h
    Human = a, c, e, f, g
2   1 = Market gardening, 2 = Dairy,
    3 = Arable, 4 = Sheep and beef

Farming in Europe

1   False
2   True
3   True
4   False
5   True
6   True
7   True
8   False
9   True
10 False

Industry

1   a = Transport, b = Labour, c = Capital,
    d = Government policy, e = Market,
    f = Raw materials
2   Primary = b, d
    Secondary = c, e
    Tertiary = f, h
    Quaternary = a, g

Industry in the UK

Correct words: a = 1800s, b = to, c = raw materials, d = Lancashire, e = 1960s, f = lost, g = modern, h = outskirts

Industry in LEDCs

1 Employment with fixed hours and wages
2 Self-employment
3 Debt repayments mean there is less money to invest in industry.
4 Transnational corporation
5 e.g. Nike
6 Advantage = b, d, e
  Disadvantage = a, c, f

Tourism

1 a = One, b = Eight, c = Thirty-six, d = Increasing, e = Decreasing
2 a = Scenery, b = Activities, c = Climate, d = Ecology, e = Culture

Tourism in the UK

1 Cumbria, England
2 d
3 b
4 b
5 a

Resources

1 True
2 True
3 False
4 True
5 False
6 False
7 True
8 True
9 False
10 True

Energy

1 Non-renewable = coal, oil, gas
  Renewable = wave, wind, solar
2 Correct words: a = 300 million years ago, b = easy, c = increasing, d = do not

Development

1 The use of resources and technology to increase wealth and improve quality of life
2 More Economically Developed Country
3 Less Economically Developed Country
4 20%
5 80%
6 Southern
7 The total value of all goods and services produced by a country in one year, divided by the total population to give an average per person.
8 The birth rate is the number of live births per thousand people per year.
9 Human Development Index
10 It combines economic and social data.

Trade

1 Exchange of goods and services
2 Goods bought by a country
3 Goods sold by a country
4 Difference between the value of the imports and exports
5 a = LEDCs, b = MEDCs, c = MEDCs, d = LEDCs, e = LEDCs, f = MEDCs

Aid

1 A transfer of resources from one country to another
2 0.7% of GNP
3 Norway, Denmark and Sweden
4 China, Egypt and Indonesia
5 a = NGO aid, b = Bilateral aid, c = Emergency aid, d = Multilateral aid, e = Long-term aid, f = Tied aid

Ecosystems

1 A collection of animals, insects, trees and plants living in a certain environment
2 Food chains
3 Between 50°N and the Arctic Circle, e.g. northern Europe to Siberia, USA and Canada
4 a = Coniferous, b = Tropical grassland, c = Desert, d = Deciduous woodland, e = Tundra

Tropical rainforests

1 Brazil, South America, West Africa, Southeast Asia
2 Agriculture, settlement, ranching, logging or mining
3 Extinction, soil erosion or global warming
4 Selective felling, helicopter transport, harvesting valuable products
5 a = Five, b = Twenty seven, c = Two thousand, d = Eighty, e = Thirty

Global warming

1 The greenhouse effect is the capture of solar energy in the atmosphere. Global warming is an increase in the average temperature of the atmosphere.
2 Carbon dioxide, methane and water vapour
3 0.6°C
4 Causes = a, c, d
   Effects = b, e, f
5 Reduce the release of carbon dioxide

Map skills

1 Contour lines, spot heights and triangulation points
2 134 metres
3 1.3 km
4 823798
5 823808

NOTES

NOTES